D1303198

MY BRAIN
MY BRAIN
MY BRAIN
MY BRAIN
MY BRAIN
MY BRAIN
MY BRAIN
HAS TOO
MANY TABS
OPEN

For Ellie and Finn, the best quaranteam.

**WHITE LION
PUBLISHING**

First published in 2021 by White Lion Publishing,
an imprint of The Quarto Group.
The Old Brewery, 6 Blundell Street
London, N7 9BH
United Kingdom
T (0)20 7700 6700
www.QuartoKnows.com

Text © 2021 Tanya Goodin

Tanya Goodin has asserted her moral right to be identified as the Author of this Work in accordance with the Copyright Designs and Patents Act 1988.

All rights reserved. No part of this book may be reproduced or utilised in any form or by any means, electronic or mechanical, including photocopying, recording or by any information storage and retrieval system, without permission in writing from White Lion Publishing.

Every effort has been made to trace the copyright holders of material quoted in this book. If application is made in writing to the publisher, any omissions will be included in future editions.

A catalogue record for this book is available from the British Library.

ISBN 978 0 71126 427 4
Ebook ISBN 978 0 71126 429 8

10 9 8 7 6 5 4 3 2 1

Designed by Louise Evans

Printed in China

MIX
Paper from
responsible sources
FSC® C016973
FSC
www.fsc.org

MY BRAIN
MY BRAIN
MY BRAIN
MY BRAIN
MY BRAIN
MY BRAIN
MY BRAIN
HAS TOO
MANY TABS
OPEN

How to Untangle Our Relationship with Tech

Tanya Goodin

LOVING (8) 12

Stories about what our tech habits are doing to our relationships

LIVING (8) 84

Stories about how our tech habits affect our daily lives

LEARNING 152

Stories about what our
tech habits are doing to
our work and our brains

✕

EPILOGUE:

INTRODUCTION

It's 1992. I am an imposter. The only woman sat in the middle of 30 men, spellbound in a dark meeting room at the Dorchester Hotel in London. A tall, thin fellow in a black polo neck is extolling the virtues of his new computer. Afterwards I share a cup of coffee with him. His presence is electric. I feel as though I'm being persuaded to join a cult. I have been an Apple fangirl ever since.

The seed that was planted during that encounter with Steve Jobs inspired me to start my own digital business in 1995. It was one of the very first in the UK, and one of very few run by a woman. Tim Berners-Lee, who starred in the London 2012 Olympic opening ceremony live tweeting the words 'This Is For Everyone', had just released the World Wide Web code, which made the internet a 'public space' accessible to everyone.
It enabled me to spend over 20 rollercoaster years at the forefront of the digital revolution. It was quite a ride.

Those early internet days were exhilarating. We were pioneers, part of the fastest technological revolution in history. Online life was simpler then. Early websites and content were either free or paid. When we paid, it was a transparent transaction where we each understood the price we were paying – and exactly what the product was.

But then came social media and persuasive technology, ad tracking and data mining, disinformation and cybercrime. We surrendered our privacy, our data and our security to enthusiastically adopt this exciting new world, without giving it a second thought. We compromised the safety of our children and unquestioningly gave up our lives to stare dumbly at our smartphones. This new era was foisted upon us at such high speed, we are all still struggling to understand what just happened.

The Industrial Revolution triggered huge social, economic and political shifts that took several hundred years to fully work themselves out. We're still at the dawn of the Digital Revolution and we don't have that long to get it right. Big Tech are now the biggest and most powerful businesses on the planet. Four of the five most valuable companies in the world are tech companies. Four of the five richest men in the world run them. And we have allowed them to write their own rules. What have we got out of this transaction? Persuasive tech has manipulated our behaviour, cybercrime has flourished in a regulatory vacuum, social media has rewarded those who speak instead of those who listen. No-one designed the digital world to produce these outcomes, but they are what a failure to think through the consequences and a Wild West attitude to policing have delivered.

We have to recapture the internet's original promise and restore Tim Berners-Lee's vision of an internet for all. We have to reclaim the technology that can be used for so much good, and regulate and restrict the monopolies that not only manipulate and track us around the internet, but also allow the darkest aspects of human nature to flourish online. By acknowledging the impacts of technology on every aspect of our daily lives, we can begin to understand, talk about and highlight those problematic experiences that are changing us. We each want to retain the incredible convenience and positive impacts of technology and social media, but instead of digital participation being a 'take it or leave it' Faustian pact, we must acknowledge the consequences of our choices and take action in our digital lives. Now is the time to reclaim our digital town squares and make them work for all of us. In this book, I highlight the ways in which we can take back control and ensure that we understand the ways in which we're being manipulated by Big Tech, as well as offering the tools to resist and change this for good.

I will always be a technophile, an early adopter, a bit of a geek. But the issues we're wrestling with today are not what I signed up for when I launched that pioneering digital business in 1995 or snapped up my first smartphone in 2007. Since 2012, it has been my mission to help individuals and businesses find a path through this unfamiliar uncharted territory. Just as I was one of the first to sign up to the promise of the digital world and see its potential,

I was also among the first to flag its newly distorted state, raising the warning cry about the possible dangers and founding 'Time To Log Off', the global digital wellbeing movement.

Some of the answers are simple and easy. Many are not. Change will only happen if we, as users, insist on it. We need technology that works for everyone, not just billionaire Big Tech owners and the mafia prospering on the Dark Web. I'm optimistic and hopeful that we can get the digital 'ecosystem' we deserve, but if we don't want our generation to be the collateral damage of this incredible Digital Revolution, we need to speak up now and start applying real pressure.

There's an important part we can all play, without waiting for changes from Big Tech. It starts with each of us taking a look at ourselves and the part we're playing in the digital world's problems. The internet shows us at our best, and at our worst. Making sure it's the former is what this book is all about.

Are you with me?

Tanya

HOW TO USE THIS BOOK

There's no right or wrong way to read this book. You can jump right in at the page that focuses on a digital dilemma you're struggling with and take it from there. But if you want to get the most out of this book, work through the three chapters in order so that you don't miss something that will help you to understand and resolve dilemmas impacting you or your loved ones. The chapters correspond with the main areas of our lives where our relationship with the digital world affects us the most. Loving is for everything to do with our relationships; Learning is for our life at work and in education (formal or otherwise); and Living is on our lives outside work.

Within each section, you'll discover a selection of stories about real people I've met and helped to improve their relationship with the digital world. In some cases, names and details have been changed to protect contributors' identities. With each dilemma, I break down the issue both for the person and for what it means for all of us, and offer practical steps you too can take if you find yourself similarly affected. From singletons looking for love or young talents climbing the career ladder, through to the lonely, disillusioned or addicted – friends, children, partners, families, everyone is included – because we are all struggling with something in our relationship with technology. All manner of digital life is contained within these pages.

This book gives you the conversation-starting vocabulary that is needed to confront and discuss these issues we're all struggling with, but also the tools to deal with them. Some of the terminology may seem unfamiliar, but the dilemmas themselves are so much a part of our daily experiences of the digital world that you will almost certainly recognize them when you read them. When we name something (an emotion, a behaviour, a problem) we start to own it.

From phubbing (ignoring a companion in favour of your phone, see page 58) to sharenting (the over-use of social media by parents to share content based on their children, see page 48), I want all of us to start using these words and owning and confronting our digital habits, so that we can have more productive conversations and start shifting the balance back to a healthy relationship with tech and the digital world, and, ultimately, with each other.

Through unpicking endlessly complicated issues from comparison culture (see page 86) to catfishing (see page 66), and by presenting real stories that demonstrate the dangers and possibilities, I hope you'll find it reassuring to know that you're not alone. Unfortunately, when Tim Berners Lee invented the World Wide Web, he didn't provide an instruction manual. I wrote this book hoping it would be the beginning of a bigger discussion on issues we're all too immersed in to see clearly. It's a wake-up call and a toolkit.

At the end of the book are my five principles for being a good digital citizen; principles that help us use the digital world in a way that keeps us healthy and happy and which guide us to take care of each other better online. Use these principles to improve, repair and enhance your relationship with technology and let them inspire you to take it a step further, to create your own personal principles for how to live your life alongside tech in the most harmonious way possible. Let's create a new wave of positivity around tech life – share your experiences of transforming your relationship with technology by using the hashtag #TooManyTabs on social media so we can all see them.

Finally, just like any instruction manual, please don't save this book only for when you have a particular problem. If some of the people you meet in this book had been able to read it a few years ago, it might have saved them a lot of trouble. Forewarned is forearmed. If you want your digital life to run smoothly you ought to know how to get the best out of it, before you encounter too many bumps in the road. I hope this book will help you do just that.

ON TECHNOFERENCE

'It's like she's in
a bubble'

The little girl, no more than nine years old, sat in the front row of the class with her hand raised. I gestured to her and smiled. 'When my Mum's on her phone,' she began hesitantly, 'it's like she's in a bubble. I try and I try, but I can't get through that bubble and get her to notice me or talk to me.'

There had been a forest of hands all waving urgently, to ask questions on the talk I had just given on using social media and staying safe online. Now I saw that they had all dropped and an expectant hush had fallen on the room. It struck me that maybe more than one of them had this problem at home.

'Well, if I was your mother standing here right now, what would you like me to know about how my phone habits make you feel?'

She paused thoughtfully before speaking.

'It makes me feel invisible. It makes me feel that I don't matter and that I'm not important.' She was talking about her heart-breaking experience in a confident, matter-of-fact tone that stung me. I had a lump in my throat as I listened to her.

'Your mother loves you very much and I think she'd be horrified to find out that this is how her phone habits are making you feel. I guarantee she doesn't realize what she's doing. She is just picking up her phone without thinking because she has got into a bad habit, not because she doesn't want to talk to you.'

She fixed my face with her eyes intently.

'I want you to promise me something. I want you to go home tonight and I want you to tell your mother exactly what you've just told me. Use exactly the same words you've just said to me.

'Maybe not when she's actually on her phone!' I added hastily to muffled laughter from the teachers at the back. 'Pick a nice quiet time, say there's something you want to talk to her about, then tell her exactly what you just told me. Will you do that?'

She nodded enthusiastically, smiling, as if my particular words were going to weave some kind of magic over her mum. I knew they would not, but I hoped the shock of them might jolt her mother into realizing she had to do something.

As I finished, the room erupted with hands being thrust up from all corners and calls of 'Miss, Miss!' It seemed everyone had a problem with a mother or a father who wouldn't, or couldn't, hear them when they needed them because they were glued to their phones. I gave them all the same answer. Go home tonight and tell your parents how their phone habits make you feel.

There are children all over the world, not just in that small London school, wondering how to tell their parents how their phone habits make them feel. In one international study, 54 per cent of children[1] said they thought their parents spent too much time on their phones, with 36 per cent saying their parents get distracted by their phones right in the middle of conversations with them, which makes them feel unimportant to them. What's most shocking about this habit is that parents appear to know exactly what they are doing. Almost half (48 per cent) of parents in a US study[2] admitted to at least three or more daily incidents of technoference in their interactions with their kids. The same US study[3] revealed that even low – or what is considered 'normal' – levels of technoference correlated with a higher level of child behaviour issues such as oversensitivity, irritability and hyperactivity. In other words, poor parenting is leading to poorly adjusted children, which should come as no surprise.

Later that night, in the very same room, I spoke to the school's parents on how to keep their children safe online. As usual there was a few minutes where I turned the spotlight on the parents themselves and asked them to think about their phone habits.

'I don't know if any of you are the parents of a little girl who spoke to me today, but I want to tell you all what she said.' I recounted the story word for word and watched them shift around uncomfortably. A father on the edge of a row dug his partner with his elbow accusingly. A mother in front turned and raised her eyebrows pointedly at her partner.

Throughout my talk to the parents that night one thing was niggling away at me. A woman sitting in the middle of the room

IT MAKES ME FEEL 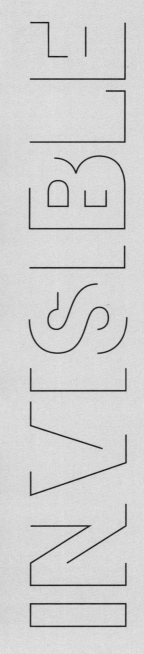INVISIBLE

54% of children think their parents spend too much time on their phones

with a face that looked familiar. I've always been useless with names but good at remembering faces. I was sure I knew her, but couldn't place her. Was she a teacher from another school I'd spoken at, come here tonight as a parent? Or a journalist I'd met recently? She was smiling at me supportively throughout.

Suddenly a memory came flooding back. I was sitting in a psychologist's office about five years before, talking about my daughter and some minor problems she was having at school. 'There's just one other thing I want you to know,' the doctor said gently, 'she says you're working on your phone a lot when you're at home. She wishes you weren't; I think she'd like a bit more of your time.'

I remembered how mortified I had been to be told this and how my cheeks had started flushing. How could I have not known that I was ignoring my own child? And yes, the woman sitting in the room that evening was the same psychologist, now with a daughter herself in the junior part of the school. And she'd come here tonight to hear me talk without realizing we had met before.

What is that old saying? 'We teach best what we most need to learn.'

I speak a lot about how addictive the devices we use every day are, the 'attention economy' where revenue is a function of continuous consumer attention, the tricks that were developed in the Persuasive Tech Lab in Stanford University that have us trapped like lab rats in a huge digital experiment. But when I speak to parents, they are always sure that it's their children who are struggling to put down their devices, never them. It's an echo of so much of our attitude towards the digital world that we think all the problems are caused by someone else. The problem of our inability to disconnect from the digital world is staring us right in the face, in the faces of our hurt and ignored children when we turn away from them for our phones.

We must do better.

Technoference:

n. a portmanteau of 'technology' and 'interference', meaning technology interference.

⚠ SIGNS:

Allowing technology to distract and interrupt you when something or someone (especially your child) needs your attention.

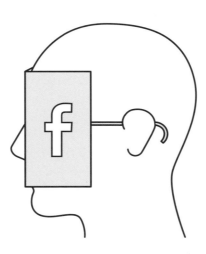

💡 SOLUTION:

You don't need me to tell you that you should put your phones down around your children. But I'll tell you why. Babies and toddlers learn their speech and communication skills from their parents. They need to see unobstructed faces to do that, not ones bowed over a phone screen. Older children need time and attention from their parents to feel secure and valued. I can't say this more forcefully; put your phone away completely when you're with your kids. Hide it in a drawer or a bag. Make it invisible in that very small window between the end of your workday and their bedtime. Don't pay lip service and keep it in your pocket, where you can still surreptitiously check it.

Make sure your children know that they are the most important people in the world to you, and that the little glass rectangle always in your hand isn't their competition. You may need to keep reminding yourself why it's so important while you're learning this new habit. Just don't let someone else have to tell you. Or, even worse, your children themselves.

ON PHADULTERY

'That one text decimated the family'

Debbie Chism reads a lot of other people's texts and WhatsApp messages. Every week, the partner in the Divorce and Family department at Stewarts in London wades through packed lever arch files full of stream-of-consciousness messages between warring partners in the high-profile divorce cases she handles.

'In the pre-digital days of divorce, people would exhibit cards or letters to support their case,' she tells me. 'Now, strings of WhatsApps and texts are exhibited as evidence and they're pretty spiky. You get extreme levels of anger that you wouldn't have got in letters or cards twenty years ago. If you wrote a letter, you probably put much more thought into it, but it's very easy to say "I hate you" in a text. Digital communication has no filter and it can be much more hurtful when it's read out in court. It looks much worse and does far more damage.'

Recriminations have always been hurled in break-ups – the end of a marriage is always painful – but the digital world is playing an increasingly important part in our relationships; not just in how they start, but how and why they break up, too. One in five American divorces now involve Facebook[1], and in Europe, 40 per cent of Italian divorces involving adultery cite WhatsApp messages as evidence[2].

Debbie has personal experience in the ways in which the digital world is affecting relationships and families, leading ever more couples to the divorce court and her door. Stewarts reported seeing a 122 per cent increase in divorce enquiries between September and December 2020. One aspect is the advent of texts and private messages.

'The digital world has made it far easier for people to get hold of their partner's private information,' Debbie explained. Text messages, WhatsApps, DMs on social media, these are all private forms of communication that can accidentally be exposed, and it happens far more frequently than, say, coming across a hidden love-letter might have happened in the pre-digital age.

Text messages have been described as the new lone blonde hair on a jacket, the new crumpled credit card bill in the pocket, which used to be tell-tale signs signalling the existence of an illicit relationship on the side. Unlike the hair strand and the bill though, a text message provides confirmation, whereas the former might have only generated suspicion. But it may not be who you think it would be stumbling across these kinds of private messages that can wreck relationships.

'You might think that coming across texts to other people by accident is fairly common, but people don't tend to pick up and check their partner's phone. They do, however, readily hand their phone to their children to use or to quickly look up some information. It's often children, who are far more tech-savvy than their parents now, who are accidentally coming across text messages that their parents have sent to others.'

Debbie told me a heart-breaking story about an 18-year-old girl who had found evidence on her father's phone that he was having a relationship, which her mother knew nothing about. 'That one text decimated the family dynamic and led to divorce.'

Family sharing apps are also causing big problems at home. Debbie handled a case where a husband had come across a private email between his wife and her doctor, which had been accidentally shared with everyone in the family, because they were all in a family sharing group. 'The loss of privacy is so easily done, the slippage of private information to the public space can cause a lot of pain.'

It's not just digital communication of the accidental kind that can cause problems in relationships. More of Debbie's clients are having to deal with the intentional use of digital communication playing a role in break-ups in what she describes as a 'spiteful and hurtful way'. 'People fake information to manipulate each other, not just pictures, but comments, posts, drip feeds of upsetting information online. They might look harmless on the surface, but they're designed to cause pain and hurt.'

We can be very cruel to each other when we're hurting ourselves. As a divorce lawyer, Debbie undoubtedly witnesses the very worst aspects of our human behaviour when she reads through WhatsApps and text messages between fighting partners, but some

WE ALL HAVE A RIGHT TO PRIVACY

of the ways in which the digital world is disrupting relationships and marriages are worth us all pausing to think about for a bit.

Texting people we shouldn't be texting, and then getting caught out, is a fairly new phenomenon, but of course having intimate relationships with people we shouldn't be, isn't. But there's something about the ease of digital communication, the immediacy and the easy familiarity of sending a text that may make it feel harmless. I can't tell you how many people I come across, who genuinely never intended to start a relationship with someone they began idly messaging, but then got 'sucked in'. Sharing intimacy by text, outside the boring mundanity of your real-world life, can be very seductive. Before you know it, you're chatting on the phone, then you're FaceTiming, eventually you're meeting up. One-third of all legal action in US divorce cases are now reported to be started as a result of affairs conducted online[3].

1 in 5
American divorces involve Facebook

Because of the digital world, what the commercial world calls the 'barriers to entry' of adultery are now pretty low. You don't even have to leave your home to engage in a relationship with someone else. You can be building the kind of intimacy that can seriously unsettle your relationship, sitting right next to your partner on the sofa. The illicit thrill of texting someone else in the company of your partner is just part of what makes it exciting and addictive. You might pass it off as 'adultery lite'... Just a bit of fun and an ego boost, not harming anyone? But as Debbie pointed out, it does very much harm someone when that information is accidentally disclosed. And sometimes the people it harms are the very ones we most want to protect: our children.

Do you know what your partner is up to online right now? *Should* you know? I can't answer that question for you; our relationships and boundaries are all different. Your views on this are probably so deeply ingrained and instinctive that you probably imagine everyone shares them and that you don't explicitly need to talk about them with your other half, but you do.

This is not about moral judgements; whatever your view on extra-marital affairs, we all have a right to privacy and to explain what privacy means to each of us. Privacy between partners, even when married, privacy about our medical affairs, privacy between us and our employer, privacy of any information we choose to keep private. The trouble is that the very nature of the digital world has debased the concept of privacy so far that we may not even be sure we have a right to it anymore. And we're increasingly careless about keeping our private information private.

The intrusion of the public view into previously private spaces has been one of the aspects of the digital world that was the most difficult to predict and yet the most taken for granted now. What Debbie described as the 'slippage' of private information into public spaces happens every day when we watch the intimate lives of total strangers on their Instagram feeds and YouTube channels. Every day we can read private texts and message being shared on sites like Reddit, or via screenshots on Twitter. Information that can identify us, expose us and even hurt us, is shared without thinking twice, despite the best efforts of cyber-security experts to tell us how we're making ourselves vulnerable.

Of course, we make ourselves vulnerable anyway when we enter a marriage or a committed relationship. We open ourselves up to our partner in many ways, not just in the digital space. But digital vulnerability and privacy must be very much on our agendas now when we think about partnering up. How can we communicate our digital needs to the person we are partnered with? How can we keep ourselves safe? How can we share with them, but still keep aspects of ourselves private? How can we resist the urge to lash out and hurt those we love(d) with the full force of the digital world at our disposal when we break up? These are not easy conversations, but they are important ones, and not just when we are parting.

Phadultery [aka cyber infidelity]:

n. engaging in an online relationship with someone other than your partner, often without actually meeting in person.

⚠ SIGNS:

Carrying out a secretive online relationship via digital means – texting, messaging, sending photos; increasing and escalating intimacy in communication, which you keep hidden from your partner.

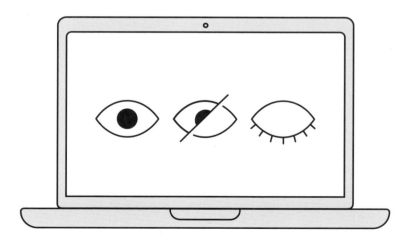

💡 SOLUTION:

In any relationship, it's important to agree what your digital couple rules are as early in the relationship as possible. Have a frank conversation about what you are comfortable with and what expectations you have of one another. Is it OK to text other people? Is it OK to accept friend requests from exes? What about your partner liking and commenting on the social media posts of an attractive third party? Are public comments OK, but DMs definitely not? What level of openness are you both prepared to have with each other about what you're doing online? Is a secret email account a 'No, No'? Does a secret dating profile ('just out of curiosity') even need discussing? Some couples share social media accounts and email addresses to reduce conflict, would you consider doing that? Would you hand your phone over, if asked? Would you never, ever, ask that of your partner, and do you expect reciprocal privacy and respect? Your rules are personal to both of you; no one else but you need know about them. Discuss and agree them.

ON FAKE NEWS

———

'He believes all
this stuff'

With the breakout session over and a coffee in hand, I could see the bank's managing director approaching me from across the room.

'It sounds a bit ridiculous, but I wondered if I could get your advice on a bit of a problem I'm having with our family WhatsApp group?'

'Sure,' I laughed.

The family WhatsApp group is a recurring theme in the Q&A at all the talks I give. Questions usually centre around how to deal with members who post non-stop trivia and memes day and night; or the thorny issue of how to leave the family group without offending everyone. (Bad news: I'm afraid my conclusion after lots of discussions on this matter is that, like the family itself, once you join a family WhatsApp group, you're in there for life.)

It turned out Mike had a very specific issue with what his brother was posting in the group, which was upsetting the rest of the family.

'He posts links to the most incredible stuff, which simply can't be true: insane news stories, conspiracy theories, fantastical plots. When he first started, we teased him or quietly ignored it, but his posts are getting more bizarre.'

Paul had posted links to 'proof' that 9/11 was staged by the US government. Now, he seemed to be immersed in the murky world of 'Q' and QAnon; a conspiracy theory based on the belief that high-ranking individuals around the world are members of a global paedophile ring. He was also getting very caught up with anti-vaxxers and Covid-deniers, who claimed that coronavirus vaccines were all part of a sinister strategy by Bill Gates to implant microchips in our brains.

Paul's grown-up children had almost completely disowned him for entertaining these unlikely theories, Mike confessed. They felt like he was beyond reasoning with, although everyone had tried. 'He believes all this stuff,' he went on, 'no one can convince him it isn't true.'

Paul's was a fairly extreme case of being taken in by, and sharing, something that's been trivialized as 'fake news'. But we've all been guilty of propelling material around the internet that isn't true. One estimate[1] claims that nearly 60 per cent of links posted on social media haven't been read by the person sharing them. (Actually, describing what we're doing online as 'reading' is a bit of a misnomer; we all scan, rather than read, and eye tracking studies[2] have shown that scanning *all* of the text on a page we're reading, or even the majority of it, is extremely rare.) We scan, the headline looks gripping, and we retweet, post or share. We're more likely to do this when we're stressed, worried or feeling under pressure. If something is making us anxious in the world, we look for quick and satisfying answers, usually for things that don't necessarily have quick and satisfying answers. Unfortunately, in doing this we're more likely to spread things that are false, than the truth. The internet is full of a variety of sources and online chat rooms that can easily 'prove' a theory and align any dots we might be looking for. It's therefore crucial that we take a step back and critically evaluate. False news has been found to travel faster and reach more people than news that is true[3]. On Twitter, news stories that are false are 70 per cent more likely to be retweeted than stories that are true[4].

It's worth unpacking for a minute exactly what we mean when we talk about what's false (not true) and what's fake (made-up) about our news online. There's 'fake news!' when it's an accusation hurled by someone in the public eye, typically against journalists whose reporting annoys them. This news is probably true but has been badly received by the subject of the story. There's misinformation, when something that's false has been posted and passed on by those who are being a bit thoughtless but don't intend to mislead anyone, a joker or a helpful relative who shares something 'just in case'. Then there's disinformation – fake information deliberately created and spread with an agenda to harm. The last two are the ones we need to be wary of, as we may be unwittingly partially responsible for its spread. In sharing disinformation in particular, and worse, believing it to be true, we're allowing ourselves to be played as pawns in a war for truth that's going on online right under our noses.

The spread of disinformation using social media is on an

exponential trajectory online. The Oxford Internet Institute has investigated its reach[5] and identified disinformation now coming out of more than 80 countries globally. This category of fake news is spread around the internet primarily using two types of accounts: automated accounts, or bots, based in huge 'troll farms' in countries such as Russia and Iran; and human-curated accounts that use low-levels of automation to engage in authentic-looking conversations online, posting, commenting and engaging with our own social media accounts and those of people we're connected to. The latter are far harder to spot as they're often framed as something chatty and pseudo-helpful such as 'a friend of a friend, working in a hospital/in government says this is what's *really* going on...'

The objectives of these 'cyber troops' deployed online to spread disinformation on behalf of their various paymasters vary hugely. Some of it can be pro-government propaganda, but much of it is anti-government, anti-establishment, anti-mainstream media, using conspiracy theories that are designed to destabilize the country or area they target by undermining confidence in those in authority. Disinformation deployed like this has a huge reach; according to research, more than 25 per cent of Americans visited a fake news website in one six-week period during the 2016 US presidential election[6]. Cyber troops spreading disinformation drives division in the country or area under attack, polarizing its citizens.

It was clear from what Mike was telling me, that Paul had fallen beyond the fairly harmless variety of false news and misinformation, into this darker place of deliberately spread disinformation and associated conspiracy theories. Psychologists think that people who are susceptible to getting drawn in by conspiracy theories share a few traits, including a tendency to being socially isolated and alienated from their community. Mike mentioned that since his divorce ten years ago, Paul had become quite reclusive and had withdrawn from his friends, preferring to spend his time at home alone, in front of his laptop. The family WhatsApp group had been part of an attempt to make him feel included, but now everyone else in the group was feeling they would be far better off without his baseless contributions. Paul's two sons had tried angrily remonstrating with him, both in and outside the WhatsApp group. But it seemed the more they told him the material he was sharing wasn't true, the more he dug his heels in and told them it was actually they who had been brainwashed by the government and media into denying the existence of a sinister deep state.

People who have come out the other side of a conspiracy theory, talk about their realization that it isn't true happening in small incremental steps, rather than one 'Ah Ha' moment of revelation. So, I explained to Mike that trying to find the perfect piece of research, article or story to refute Paul's beliefs once and for all wasn't going to work. Neither was being angry and confrontational. If you think of falling for disinformation and conspiracy theories as being akin to brainwashing, you can see how you have to take a longer term and more systematic approach.

I asked Mike if he thought he could explain to the rest of the family that they had to try and be sympathetic towards Paul's worries about the world, which came from a place of feeling disconnected, and that he was probably turning to the extremist views he found online for a sense of meaning and belonging and to make sense of what was going on around him in the world which increasingly worried and frightened him. They needed to make him feel more included in the family, not less, especially when he posted something outlandish. I'd noticed the people who were posting the more extreme conspiracy theories in my own network often lived alone, and were spending a disproportionate amount of time online, getting lost in the darker side of the internet.

Mike's plan, as he formulated it while we talked, included suggesting some regular cycle rides with Paul, something they had always enjoyed doing when they were younger, and maybe training for a longer charity ride to raise money for a local hospital Paul had always supported. At the very least, this would get him out of the house and away from his laptop. Mike also hoped it might

More than 25% of Americans visited a fake news website during the 2016 US presidential election

reconnect Paul with the real-world community outside his door, removing him from the darker aspects of the online community he was getting hooked in to.

Seeing wild stories spread online can inspire mockery and can feel harmless if you reduce the silliness to sense. But those who are vulnerable can be taken in by things we may be able to easily see are demonstrably fake. And conspiracy theories that attack those working in our communities to keep us safe can do a lot of harm. Medical professionals working in coronavirus wards were subject to waves of abuse from Covid-deniers online, accusing them of

the
WAR ON
TRUTH

'lying' about the situation in their hospitals, which had a serious psychological impact on them at a time when they were under huge pressure. Do we want those protecting us to be treated like this?

And as for protecting us, where have tech companies been while lies and false information has been allowed to spread online and do such harm? Propaganda has always existed in history but, thanks to social media, now the cost barriers to producing false information are low and the global reach of it is huge. Facebook's promotion of groups perfectly aligned with the growth of QAnon and their message, while WhatsApp and Telegram groups have become the perfect vehicle for those sharing dark theories about the 'Great Reset' and the NWO (New World Order). It would not be cynical to feel dismayed and shocked by the suspiciously slow response to dangerous notions that feed the multiple clicks and engagement that makes them billions. Each giant insists that this is an industrial-scale problem and that they are working as fast as they can, so have they lost control? Or are these mammoth-sized, richest companies in the world not throwing all their ingenuity and power behind this? The enabled result is a digital cesspit where facts and the truth are often irreparably damaged and debased, and families are torn apart.

While we wait for them to clean up their act, watching others fall down the dark hole of false and fake information online may feel like it's really not our problem. But communities both online and off need gatekeepers, and we all need to fight against lies spreading online. We can do our part by paying much more attention to what we're reading and sharing. One study that should encourage us showed that when people did take the time to stop and think about news stories, they improved at working out what was true, whether or not their politics and beliefs matched with the news being shared[7]. We can all be part of an effective defence in the war on truth if we pause, think and stop sharing things that aren't true. Actually, if we stopped sharing anything at all the tsunami of disinformation would dry up. It's us that are spreading it after all.

Fake News [aka Misinformation]:

n. false or inaccurate information that is communicated regardless of an intention to deceive.

⚠ SIGNS:

There are two types of fake news: stories that aren't true and stories that have some element of truth but aren't 100 per cent accurate. Distinguishing between the two is tricky, but the latter can be more dangerous. Three clues that a piece of information might be false include: (1) The website: check the url, is it a regular domain like .com .org or something a bit odd like .com. co? (2) The author: is the author named and can you find their details elsewhere, or is it anonymous? (3) The story: can you cross-check the claims in the story on a reputable site or have you seen it reported on the TV or in other media?

💡 SOLUTION:

As an absolute minimum read the content behind every link you share. Develop a critical mindset. Do your homework on the people whose views you are sharing (they might have other agendas). Research sources and evidence and cross-check against reputable news sites, or even Wikipedia. The BBC's Reality Check team fact-checks stories trending across various platforms. Work out how the story makes you feel; if it generates a strong emotional response, dig deeper. We're often prompted to share things that make us angry. Agents of disinformation prey on this. If in any doubt, don't share.

If someone you know is sharing misleading or false information, try a non-judgemental approach; avoid sweeping dismissals like 'you're wrong' or 'that's ridiculous'; try not to judge; make an effort to get to the concern at the bottom of the conspiracy or disinformation they're sharing. Present them with facts and research by all means (try and do it neutrally), but understand that emotions are involved, so facts and logic often have no impact. Make a connection with them and try and engage with them that way. Listen to others who offer an opinion and be tolerant. Be patient with them and with yourself.

ON FLAKY FRIENDS

'The loneliness is
like an ache'

Helen had slipped her coat on and had her door keys in her hand when the text notification buzzed on her phone.

'Sorry babe, full-on day at work, not going to be able to make it, can we refix? Call tomorrow xoxo.'

She felt a weight descending on her shoulders as she slumped down onto the staircase in the shared hallway. Not again.

She had had a feeling this was going to happen. As the day wore on, she had been checking her phone more frequently. As she started getting ready for the evening, she had allowed herself to hope; but there it was. The last-minute cancellation. Again.

'It's the third time in the last couple of weeks,' she told me, 'and it's not even the same person every time. It's everyone. No one seems to think twice about cancelling at the last minute anymore. I'd never tell them, but sometimes the loneliness is like an ache.'

Helen is a successful marketing manager in her late 20s and lives on her own. She has watched friends settle down and start families around her, but her social life has always been lively and fulfilling. Drinks out, trips to see a movie, meals with friends. However, a slow paradigm shift in commitment and accountability has made her last two years unbearably lonely. Of course, that stage of life is a time of big changes in so many areas, not least in respect to our friends. We may be watching them settling down, building their families and striking out in new career directions. It could be that tech is compounding an already tricky time for Helen. But I have heard this complaint across all the age groups, from teens to those in their 40s and 50s.

I blame the enigmatic 'maybe' button on Facebook Events. Reinvented in 2015 as the supposedly less elusive 'interested', but known to all of us as the 'I probably won't' cop-out option.

Facebook originally invented the 'maybe' button as a way to increase engagement on the platform (you'll have heard this as a motivation for a feature before). It was perfectly geared towards the indecisive, actively encouraging passivity and passing this off as meaningful engagement. The idea was that if you checked 'maybe' you indicated your broad interest and would still get updates about the event in your feed. In reality, it became a global excuse for flaking. Too embarrassed to take the hard-line 'no' option unless we had a cast-iron excuse, or perhaps too indifferent or lazy to really consider offering ourselves to the commitment, we all checked 'maybe' to look like the motivated and supportive friend, colleague or family member we hoped everyone knew us to be. Then didn't turn up.

Changing 'maybe' to 'interested' was supposedly designed to make it less ambiguous as to who was intending to attend. It does read as a weak 'yes' but only marginally trumps the faintly defiant 'what's in it for me?' tone of 'maybe'. In reality, the change from 'maybe' to 'interested' was inconsequential. A survey of 2,000 Americans revealed the average person fails to attend half (46 per cent) of all the events they're invited to, and more than half (51 per cent) of millennials in the same survey said they have actually accepted an invitation up front with little to no intention of ever attending[1]. A few 'techiquette' ground rules are overdue and need to be laid down. If we click 'yes' to the invitation, unless we're run over on the night, we're going.

Technology in all its guises is making flakes out of all of us. FOBO (Fear of a Better Option), the sinister sibling of FOMO (Fear of Missing Out), has us analysing all the various options that might be open to us, succumbing to analysis paralysis and often choosing none of them. The swipe culture of online dating, for example, has spawned ghosting and benching and orbiting, where everyone circles around each other, keeping their options open in case they miss a really big prize among the millions of online daters. It has turned the search for love into a commodity.

Commitments are cheapened because technology is enabling us to get out of them so easily. I've done it, you've done it. The chances are everyone reading this has cancelled on a friend last minute, sending a quick text, DM or WhatsApp message, then putting our phone away quickly before we could feel guilty about it. You don't even have to hear the disappointment in someone's voice when you cancel. Technology allows us to opt out of all accountability.

The technology that was supposed to connect us is contributing to a modern-day loneliness epidemic. 9 per cent of adults in Japan, 22 per cent in America and 23 per cent in Britain say they 'always or often' feel lonely, lack companionship or feel left out or isolated[2]. And it's not the elderly, but those under 35 – the heaviest users of technology and social media – who are the loneliest of all. A study of Americans aged 19–32 found those who used social media most often were more than twice as likely to report loneliness as those using it least[3].

Social media also presents us with the reassuring illusion of feeling connected, while permitting us to stay distant and isolated. Leaving likes and comments on our friends' social media posts and stories, sending a chain of text messages and memes throughout the week; these all make us feel we're staying in touch and investing time and effort into our nearest and dearest. We tell ourselves that we're fully involved in our friends' lives, that we're all caught up with what's going on with them. But what we're doing is keeping superficial ties and connections, we're not building and reinforcing deep bonds. Six in 10 British adults in a 2019 survey admitted they spent less time catching up with friends since the world became more digital, with 55 per cent saying that social media has made their relationship with mates 'more superficial'[4].

Professor Robin Dunbar, British anthropologist and evolutionary psychologist, says, 'The more close relationships you have, the higher your levels of happiness are. Making small changes to our lifestyles like cutting down on social media can give us more time and space in the "real world" to embrace convivial moments with friends. And doing this is what creates close, fulfilling and happy friendships.' These small changes, like arranging physical meetings and socialising with our friends and family, raise our own happiness levels and strengthen our ties. It requires more effort than a simple message, but the benefits are enormous.

51% of millennials accept an invitation with no intention of attending

I asked Helen if she had ever told any of the friends who cancelled on her how she felt about it. Or how upset and lonely she felt when it happened so often. She looked uncomfortable.

'Oh no, I always say it's fine...'

'So how is anyone to know that all this last-minute cancelling is actually a problem?' I queried.

We sat in silence for a while, as Helen digested this.

Helen went away from our chat resolved to be more honest with her friends about how their cancelling really made her feel. And to do better herself. She thought one problem might be that all her friends were over-committing themselves, unable to look at the blank white squares in the calendars on their phones without panicking that they needed to be filled. Maybe social media, with its illusion of everyone leading action-packed and exciting lives was partly to blame here. Maybe, FOMO was making them all say 'yes' to every invitation, without thinking them through, leaving them more likely to cancel?

It's become increasingly difficult to leave ourselves time to do nothing. By being tethered to our smartphones and buying into the 'always on' culture, our free time is being monetized and overstimulated. We're unwittingly tethering ourselves to the attention economy and the bi-product of this is over-committing ourselves to the point where we don't have the energy to fulfill all of our commitments. Something has to give, and perhaps simply saying 'no' to an invitation is the best way to give ourselves time to unwind instead of trying to fit everything in. In the pandemic, many of us found ourselves experiencing what a completely unscheduled life looks like. Maybe fully appreciating the unexpected pleasures of all that space and time will make saying no a little bit easier.

We can't blame technology for all our shortcomings. The people that are cancelling on us with last-minute texts, clicking 'interested' but then not turning up, might be the ones that are letting us down in the non-digital world, too. Why are they still our friends? Don't we deserve something better? If we value real connection and meaningful relationships, we have to find others who value those too. Let's stop making excuses for others. If they bail on us, let's bail them out of a relationship that's not rewarding for either of us. Let's look closely at ourselves and make sure we're not making the same mistakes, and if we need time to ourselves, let the person know and politely decline. It's better to be upfront at the beginning than simply dropping out at the last minute or not showing up. The ease and convenience of technology comes with a price. We should not pay the price with our friends.

Flaky Friends:

n. unreliable friends, friends who make plans with you then cancel, letting you down.

⚠ SIGNS:

Habitually receiving (or sending) cancellations for planned social events at the very last minute, usually via a text.

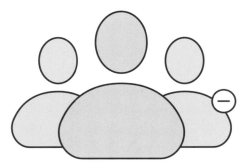

💡 SOLUTION:

Don't let technology enable your flakiness. Have some accountability for your actions instead of sweeping it under the carpet and ignoring any possible fall-outs. Don't accept each and every invitation that is extended to you without assessing if you realistically can – or even want to – attend. The time spent thinking about your decision to attend up front, will save any angst later on when you deliberate on whether to cancel or not. Watch out for any people-pleasing tendencies you might have. You're going to upset many more people when you let them down at the last minute, than when you explain you can't accept their invitation up front. If you absolutely must cancel, pick up the phone (I can't stress this enough). Never, ever cancel via text. 'Good news via text, bad news via voice' is my rule. Let them hear your voice, listen to theirs, convey your regret properly. Ensure there are no hurt feelings in order to safeguard your relationship. If you're cancelling on someone who lives alone, for whom this may be a big deal, think more than twice about last-minute flaking. Put yourself in their shoes. How would you feel? One day, it might be you.

ON SHARENTING

'He embarrasses me'

'**P**lease, can you have another word with Dad about it?'
Sitting in a packed theatre, squeezed in like sardines, I couldn't help but overhear the conversation behind me between a girl and her mother waiting for the show to start.

'But, it's a lovely photo of you', her mother protested, in a distracted voice, rummaging in her bag for her theatre programme.

'I hate it, but that's not the point,' came the retort.

As their chat unfolded, it transpired that what was causing the upset was not a particular photo of the girl, but the very many photos of her that were being taken by her father and tagged and uploaded to his Facebook account.

'I keep telling him not to do it, but he just ignores me. He embarrasses me with all the stuff he uploads.'

One recent complaint was the plastering of old baby photos on his Facebook page for her fourteenth birthday, compiled for an 'I can't believe she's all grown up' photo montage.

I could tell from the noises her mother was making that she wasn't taking the conversation very seriously.

'I'll tell him again, but don't give him too hard a time. It's just Dad being Dad, all parents want to show their kids off,' she added, as their conversation was brought to an abrupt end by the curtain going up on the show.

I overhear people having conversations about their phone habits all the time and I'd heard this particular one before. At a primary school I'd listened in as a group of younger kids teased each other about something one of their parents had posted online. On more than one occasion, I'd had teenagers asking me how they could ask their grandparents to stop posting photos of them online, on accounts that had no privacy settings. First coined by the *Wall Street Journal* in 2012[1] and one of *Time*'s 'words of the month' in February 2013, sharenting as a habit is admitted to by 42 per cent of UK parents[2] who say they share photos of their children online, with the average parent sharing almost 1,500 images of their child online before their fifth birthday[3]. More than 81 per cent of children are said to have an online presence by the age of two[4], thanks to the enthusiastic activities of their parents.

Each time I'd had a conversation about this, I could see that what was so exasperating was that the young people felt their requests weren't being taken seriously. Parents, brought up in the analogue camera era, saw social media posts as the equivalent of the family photo album that their own parents had brought out at embarrassing moments. Their children, who have had cyber-safety lessons drilled into them almost from birth, knew that it was very different. More than that, often parents felt they had a 'right' to post about their children if they wanted to. And their children definitely disagreed. Research in the US[5] showed that 19 per cent of parents acknowledged they have posted something online that their child may find embarrassing in the future. Additionally, 13 per cent of parents say that their child has already been embarrassed by something they have posted, and 10 per cent say their child has asked them to remove an online post that relates to them.

In 2016, an 18-year-old woman from Austria even brought a case against her parents to try and force them to remove childhood pictures of her from Facebook. In France, stringent privacy laws mean that parents are legally responsible for protecting images of their children, so they too could find themselves the subject of future legal actions, if they breach their children's privacy online.

That Austrian teenager said of her parents: 'They knew no shame and no limits, they didn't care if I was sitting on the toilet or lying naked in the cot, every moment was photographed and made public,' she said, stressing that the pictures were not only embarrassing but were a violation of her privacy. The young woman said she had repeatedly asked her parents to remove over 500 pictures of her from Facebook, but they had refused. So, she decided to take legal action against them as soon as she turned 18.

'I'm tired of not being taken seriously by my parents,' she said.

If all our children go down this route, our courts are going to be busy for decades. So, let's start listening to their entreaties to protect their privacy, instead of seeing it as shyness, vanity or fussing unnecessarily?

As they grow, children understand how much their offline and online identities are entwined, and they care very much about how they are portrayed in the digital world. Social media profiles are identity projects for teens and young people and they construct them carefully. Adding unwanted images of them breaks the trust between the parent and the child they want to protect. In 2015, Gwyneth Paltrow sparked an online debate on sharenting when she upset her daughter Apple by posting family selfies taken on a skiing trip without the latter's permission. The 14-year-old remonstrated publicly: 'Mom, we have discussed this. You may not post anything without my consent.' Children want and deserve to have control over their own image.

Sonia Livingstone, Professor in the Department of Media and Communications at the London School of Economics and Political Science, spends much of her time focusing on children's rights in the digital age. She told me:

'Research for my book *Parenting for a Digital Future* shows that parents are really torn – they do care about their children's privacy, and they are increasingly aware that what they post can stay online forever and might have future consequences. On the other hand, they really want to share *their experiences* of parenting with family and friends, and this is important for their own self-expression and sense of connection with others, not just as an individual but *as a parent*, a role crucial to their identity. Children, however, are increasingly vocal that they want to be *asked*, whether to give or withhold consent, and they especially don't want to be portrayed in a way that embarrasses them. In resolving this conundrum, it's heartening that families are trying to recognize each other's point of view. It would help to have more usable privacy settings, and to be able to permanently remove content later when circumstances or consent changes.'

More than **81%** of children have an online presence by the age of two

The sheer volume of material that parents post, motivated by the best intentions of parental pride, may have the unintentional risk of leaving children open to online fraud and identity theft later in life. Imagine location-tagging a photo, posted by you, a mother who hasn't changed your name through marriage, featuring a birthday boy on the day of his 7th birthday, wearing his favourite football team's shirt with the much-loved family pet by his side, name visible on the dog-tag. You will have made available several valuable pieces of identifying data in one photo: date of birth, possibly place of birth, favourite team, name of pet, mother's maiden name. Sophisticated face-recognition software, which already exists, will associate all that information with the many thousands of photos that will reside online of your child by the time he becomes an adult, and prove a godsend for fraudsters. Sharenting has been described as the 'weakest link' in risking online fraud and identity theft, with one forecast estimating that the practice could lead to 7.4 million incidents per year of identity theft by 2030, costing almost £670m in online fraud[6].

As far as our babies and toddlers are concerned, social media companies have brainwashed us into thinking their platforms are the ideal repository for photos of our families. They are no such thing. They are advertising networks, focused on keeping us coming back to their site time and time again. They can be hacked, and images can be captured, downloaded and stolen. They are the very worst place to store photos of young children. Naked photos of babies and children are routinely harvested by paedophile websites and spread across the internet. Reports suggest that paedophilic websites have been discovered to have stolen over half their photos from family posts on social media sites like Facebook[7]. Material of this kind is searched for, replicated and shared every day. Even relatively innocent photos of young children in swimsuits can be doctored for obscene purposes by overlaying text and speech bubbles. Is this what you want to happen to your precious memories of your children? These photos are online forever and once posted, their use is beyond your control.

I don't always get to hear the resolution of a dilemma like the one that unfolded behind me in the theatre that night. This girl had tried to talk to both of her parents about this before, but her mother was dismissing it as just another bit of teenage angst.

If this conversation presents itself to you, pay attention. This is not an issue that need only concern you if you're a parent, either. Consent is an ethical obligation for all of us. Consenting to a photo of us being taken, and shared, is our right. The next time you try and corral a friend into a group photo on a night out, or upload a picture of them that they say they don't like: Stop. There's a huge pressure on all of us, at all ages, to be constantly visible online. Sometimes those we love may want to opt out of all of that for a while, for reasons of their own. You may even want to at some point, too. Don't put the onus on those who don't want to be tagged or photographed to bring it up. Always ask permission. Always get consent. When someone says 'No', don't do it. No further questions asked.

YES

Always get consent.

NO

When someone says 'No', don't do it.

Sharenting:

v. a combination of 'over-sharing' and 'parenting'; the over-use of social media by parents to share content based on their children, such as baby pictures or details of their children's activities. Related to the concept of TMI ('too much information').

⚠ SIGNS:

Posting an endless stream of photos of your children and/or every conceivable detail of all their many and varied achievements, from their success at potty training and weaning, up to their high school graduation and first kiss.

💡 SOLUTION:

Don't ever share photos of very young children on social media. If you need to share photos remotely with relatives, set-up a family photo-sharing account in the cloud. Even then, remember, every account can be hacked. Never put anywhere online bath shots or pictures of your child unclothed. Avoid posting information that can be harvested for identity fraud at a later stage in life, such as precise dates of birth, the house number, their mother's maiden name, their place of birth, the name of their first pet, favourite sports teams etc. Give older children the power of veto over the posting online of any images or information about them. Listen to their concerns, without dismissing them. Apart from their embarrassment, material posted by you may come back to haunt them at some stage in their lives or careers, so it's important to take it seriously. Be conservative and cautious on their behalf. Your goal should be to get them to the age of around 16 entirely invisibly online. If you can do that, you're giving them a gift far greater than your proud boasts about their milestones and achievements and will set them up for the beginning of a safe online future.

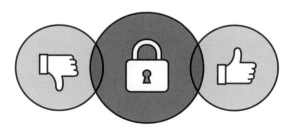

ON PHUBBING

'There are three of us
in this relationship'

A coder met me at reception, and gestured with his head to the hand sanitiser bottle fixed to the wall. This happened to be my first sanitiser experience and the very last company talk I gave in March 2020, before lockdown hit the UK.

It was a warehouse-style open-plan office in trendy Shoreditch, East London. There was one of those clichéd metallic shoot-style slides between the two floors, and a bunch of games tables in the corner next to glass-fronted fridges rammed with energy drinks. The entirely 20-something workforce were all sitting at their desks in front of me, headsets plugged in, tapping away silently at their keyboards.

The woman who bounded up to me was in her 40s. I recognized her instantly from the photo on their website. This was Kat, the founder of the business.

'Great, you're here! There's something I want to talk to you about quickly, before you kick off.'

She launched into an explanation about how she had set the company up with her husband, James – she ran the sales and marketing and was the 'face' of the business and he was focused on operations, the network and IT support.

'I have a problem with James, and I need you to cover it, without him knowing we've spoken.'

This was a new one on me. I had never actually been asked to do any kind of marriage counselling before, let alone the kind where one partner wanted their concerns to be communicated entirely subliminally to the other.

'So, the problem with James is,' she sighed, 'he literally never puts his phone down. At night, when we've got home and we're crashing on the sofa, he has it permanently glued to his hand. There are three of us in this relationship and the third is his phone! It's driving me demented. Can you say anything about that, without making it obvious it's directed at him?'

I reassured her that I absolutely could, and would, cover what we now call 'phubbing' (a particularly unimaginative combination of the words 'phone' and 'snubbing'). I'm sure you've experienced this as many times as I have. There you are, happily chatting to your friend or partner in a bar or over dinner or a coffee, and mid-sentence, without missing a beat in their stream of words, they pick up their phone and start scrolling through it right in front of you.

Over one-third of all of those in a relationship in the UK say they have been ignored by their phone-distracted partners[1]. Millennials, aged 25–34, were reported to be the worst perpetrators of the act, with 57 per cent complaining that the habit affected their romantic lives. In the US, prevalence appears even higher, with 70 per cent of people in a relationship reporting they have been 'phubbed' by their partner[2]. Leading on from this, 22 per cent of people in those relationships say they have then experienced 'conflict' as a direct result (probably a blazing row). This may not be as unconscious a habit as it seems as 71 per cent of millennials in the US admit they have actively used their smartphones to avoid a social interaction[3].

Of course, it's not just romantic partners who inflict this habit on each other, friends and colleagues are just as guilty of it. When it happens to me, I always want to shout out, 'Sorry, am I *boring* you?' But phubbing is much less about how entertaining or compelling our company is, and much more about the impulse control of the other person.

How often you 'phub' has been linked to how good you are at self-control generally. If you struggle with resisting urges in other areas of your life, you're going to struggle not to check your phone. It also seems to be a reciprocal habit. If we see other people checking their phones around us, we're more likely to think it's acceptable, and join in. There are lots of people who evidently do think it's OK to pick up a phone and check it mid-conversation. I'm not one of them. Think back to how you felt when someone last did it to you.

Smartphones were designed to keep us connected with those physically distant from us, but they're undermining our connection with those we're actually with. They pull us out of the present and take us to another place, depriving us of the opportunity right here, right now, to make a real connection.

His phone is
permanently

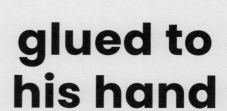

glued to
his hand

71% of millennials in the US consciously use their smartphones to avoid a social interaction

When we 'phub' in our intimate relationships something else is going on, too. We're avoiding intimacy. We're deflecting our partner's bids for attention. We're keeping them at arm's length, in our moments of togetherness. A generation ago we might have buried our head in a newspaper, pretending not to hear.

Unsurprisingly, it's not making anyone any happier; two recent studies found that when spouses 'phub' each other, they're more likely to experience depression and lower marital satisfaction[4].

Our digital devices have become our excuses not to connect, symbols of our unwillingness to hear. To build genuine connection we need to lower the barriers they allow us to erect between each other. Treating each other with kindness involves us always making the active decision to prioritize the person standing in front of us, whoever they are, not the smartphone in our hand.

The presentation to Kat and her team went well; they were a surprisingly animated bunch once they took their headphones off. Kat was sitting on my right as I faced the audience and when I got to the part about phubbing, she smiled knowingly, nodding her head up and down emphatically. I shot a nervous glance at James who was off to my left to see how he was taking it but luckily, he was also smiling. Clearly utterly oblivious to his own bad habits, I thought.

Afterwards, they had organized beers and snacks for the team and invited me to stay and join them, so I put my kit aside and made my way over to the crowd gathered around the games tables.

Kat was talking to her PR manager in the corner of the room and I was feeling a little bit lost among the coders until James bounded up to me and pressed a cold drink into my hand.

'That was great' he enthused, 'really loved everything you had to say!

'Especially,' he leaned in conspiratorially, 'the bit about phubbing. Kat has a real problem with it. She just can't put her phone down, especially when we're at home together. It drives me absolutely mad.'

Kat looked over to see where I was, caught James' eye, and they smiled at each other across the room.

Phubbing:
v. the act of ignoring a companion, usually your intimate partner, in favour of your phone.

⚠ SIGNS:

Picking up and scrolling or messaging on your phone, while your partner or companion is talking. Unable to resist the urge to check your phone when 1-2-1 with your partner.

☼ SOLUTION:

Phubbing damages relationships. It's not a good sign if it's happening in yours, so don't trivialize it. If it happens to you, stop dead in your tracks and don't say another word until your partner puts their phone down. Smile, but keep your lips completely sealed. (You could say, 'It's OK, I'll wait,' if they indicate they want you to carry on talking while they scroll.) You don't need to remonstrate or nag to change this bad habit, you just have to reward positive behaviour with a little nudge. This nudge works a treat. If you're the guilty party, my rule is '**No Phones 1-2-1**'. Make your phone invisible when it's just you and one other person. Even if the other person's phone is out on the table or sofa in front of you both, put yours away. It means the act of starting to reach into your pocket or bag to find it may pull you up and stop you from going any further.

Because this habit is reciprocal, I've found that others now automatically put their phones away around me, too. Protect and preserve the space between you and your partner where you connect, and don't let a phone come between you.

ON CATFISHING

———

'Someone is pretending
to be you'

Max Benwell was lying in bed one morning in March 2018 in his New York apartment, browsing through Twitter, when he noticed a late-night DM.

'Hey, I just wanted to let you know that someone is pretending to be you.'

He had no idea who the woman was, so he decided to ignore it, but a couple of weeks later he received a message from another woman, then a third:

'Someone has been using your photos to catfish me.'

'There is someone on the internet who stole your photos and is using them to try and catfish people.'

Suddenly, Max realized that he might have a problem on his hands.

'Catfishing' as a term has its roots in a 2010 US documentary 'Catfish', where Nev Schulman charts his experience developing a messaging relationship with an attractive 19-year-old young woman via a dating site, who turns out to be a 40-year-old housewife with multiple fake online identities. The husband of the housewife inspired the term, when he mentioned how catfish and cod act differently when alone or apart in tanks.

Max, then a 27-year-old journalist, set off on his own journey to try and track down the person who was using his photos. Thanks to his professional skills, his ingenuity, the setting up of several fake social media accounts, changing his gender on Tinder, and the help of California-based social media investigation service Social Catfish, he eventually tracked the catfisher, Chris, down.

It wasn't just that Chris was using photos of Max, it was the fact that Chris was unleashing a stream of vile abuse at the women he was catfishing; all of which was accompanied by Max's grinning face as the avatar. The impact that this must have had on the targeted women is sickening. What it also does is highlight that the victims in catfishing scenarios are both the women concerned *and*, in this case, Max. The women are abused, whilst the abuse is attributed to Max's face across the internet. He felt angry and mortified:

'I wanted to make him feel some shame for what he had done,' he told me. 'To say to him "these are real people, what you're doing has had real life consequences".'

Max chatted to Chris for over an hour on the phone. About the same age as Max and still living with his parents, Max said, 'He was obviously panicking, and I did feel a bit sad for him wondering what would make him do that. But then, I didn't feel I was the real victim. I thought about all the women who were affected by this.' Max had already asked some lawyers whether catfishing was a crime in the US, 'but they told me it was incredibly hard to get the police involved: unless you can prove financial or reputational damage, catfishing rarely gets prosecuted.'

After his phone confrontation with Chris, Max decided to stop pursuing him. 'Chris could still be doing it, but I realized I would go mad if I spent every day trying to find out if my photos were still being used somewhere. I felt trying to track them down and get them all removed would be like trying to stop a ship full of holes sinking.'

Social Catfish had found that Max's photos were not just being used by Chris on a dating platform, but were also being used by two people for their Yelp reviews, as a profile photo for someone on a freelance working website, and even by a man selling shoes. Because Max is a journalist, he thinks his pictures had probably been found and used as a result of his work. 'But you don't even need to be that active on social media now for it to happen to you,' he said. 'I do know people who are proud that they can't be found online, but everyone should be free to join and use social media without worrying about this happening to them.'

How many of you reading this book right now have clones of yourself floating around the internet, using your smiling face to give any range of shady activities an aura of authenticity? Can any of us be sure? Identity has always been a loosely defined concept online. There's no such thing as a digital passport, or an ID card, to verify you as you move around the internet. False identities

IDENTITY

IDENTITY

IDENTITY

IDENTITY

IDENTITY

IDENTITY

IDENTITY

£63m was lost by UK victims of romance fraud in 2020

are frighteningly easy to assume online, and so-called romance, or dating, fraud where fake identities are used for very specific financial purposes on dating websites, has been cited as one of the fastest growing types of cybercrime. Americans reported losses of over \$201 million in 2019 to romance scams[1], and in the UK, victims of online romance fraud were conned out of more than £63 million in 2020, up from the £50 million lost in 2018[2]. More than one in 10 UK adults have now been the victim of a romance scam and it's one of the most difficult areas of fraud to tackle, largely because so many people who have fallen victim to it are embarrassed to admit to it, or even discuss it. Two-thirds of UK victims (62 per cent) said they had been too embarrassed to admit it had happened to them, to their friends and family – or even to the authorities[3].

When identity or romance fraud involves attempts to extract money, it can be much more difficult to detect than the activities of an online pariah misrepresenting themself. Dedicated romance fraudsters are much more sophisticated than catfisher Chris. These days sophisticated AI chat bots can look incredibly real and can carry out a complex conversation with you that looks and feels just like the real thing.

How are any of us to know if someone is really who they claim to be online? Gut feeling, reading body language, noticing subtle inconsistencies, and our instinct, all work far better in person than they do via text and photographs or video. We've had thousands of years of evolution to help us 'read' someone standing right in front of us, but a mere few decades working out how to do that on a screen, and in the case of dating, only since the launch of the first dating websites in the mid 1990s.

As a minimum, all of us need to do our research on anyone we might be talking to online. This is a tricky area, as anyone who has ever heard the words, 'I googled you' will know. Realizing that someone has been looking you up online has an intrusive, slightly stalkerish feel to it, even though we all know that absolutely everyone googles absolutely everyone else. But a few simple searches, verifying basic details of names and background, takes just minutes and could help you uncover anything obvious.

There are some clear signs that we can try and look out for in order to spot a catfisher early. If they ask lots of questions but quickly shut down questions about themselves, make up excuses not to meet up in person (working offshore on an oil rig or being posted with the military overseas are favourites), tell elaborate stories as to why they need money, or their pictures seem too perfect (usually because they are lifted from an online modelling portfolio somewhere), they may well be a fake account. Internet searches on the name and background will draw blanks, which your catfisher may explain as 'being private' or 'not really being into social media'. Always take a step back and try and evaluate the situation, and speak to friends for their opinion if you think something may seem suspicious.

We also need to accept when we might be at our most vulnerable and susceptible to identity and romance fraud, so that we are even more vigilant at these times. Max told me that his investigations suggested that 'middle-aged women on Facebook, recently separated or divorced' are prime targets. Indeed, fraud data does show that a high proportion of romance fraud victims are lonely, widowed or recently bereaved, have suffered from a recent break-up and/or are suffering from depression[4].

There really is no substitute for meeting and getting to know someone face-to-face to judge whether they are who they claim to be, and even that isn't foolproof of course. Drawn-out texting relationships can feel a lot less scary than taking the step to meet someone in person, but they run the risk of making you feel you know and trust (and in some cases, even love) someone before you've ever met them.

People sometimes misrepresent themselves not to abuse or exploit others, but for less harmful reasons. This could be because of their insecurities, loneliness or wanting to have a safe way to explore their sexuality. They might misrepresent their appearance as in 'hatfishing' (hiding your baldness under a hat in dating photos). But whatever the reason, it isn't fair to mislead others. It's not fair on the women Chris contacted who were duped and then subjected to abuse. It's not fair on Max, whose face and identity these messages were attributed to. Where your heart is concerned, and until better methods exist to verify online identity, trust your in-person human instinct, finely honed over millennia, rather than giving too much of yourself, too soon, to the flirty messaging and seductive profile pics of cyberspace. Be cautious, be safe, be smart.

Catfishing:

v. the act of pretending to be someone you are not online, in order to lure someone you've never met into a relationship, or to defraud a victim in some way.

⚠ SIGNS:

A catfisher's photos may seem unusually perfect and they can be reluctant to take part in video calls or meet up in person. If you are being prepped for financial fraud, the conversation will turn to money, with an emotive story about a problem that is leaving them short of it. If you have never visited their home, workplace or met anyone else who knows them, they may be married or in an existing relationship.

☀️ SOLUTION:

Recognizing you're being conned or scammed while dating is hard; admitting it to someone else is even harder. Don't be embarrassed if you think you might have fallen for something or someone that is fake, it's happened to a surprising number of people. The most important thing is to talk about it. Share any concerns with a trusted third party, as soon as any doubts arise. Always be wary of someone who has an elaborate reason not to meet up, has a far-flung job or is proposing a long-distance relationship. Never, ever transfer money or identifying financial or personal information to someone you haven't ever met in person, no matter how plausible or convincing their excuse for not being able to meet. A reverse image search on Google Images can tell you if photos posted aren't of the person who claims to be talking to you, but it isn't foolproof. (Go to images.google.com, click the camera icon and either paste in the URL for an image you've seen online, upload an image from your hard drive, or drag an image from another location.)

Adopt an approach of caution (aka cynicism) in all online dating encounters, until you have met up in person with those you are messaging (and even then, until you have got to know them much better). If you have recently experienced a loss, or are suffering from depression, you are especially vulnerable when online dating so proceed carefully.

ON DIGITAL LEGACIES

'Like visiting a place we
used to hang out'

Amit was distracting himself on his phone after midnight, a few days before his best friend Ishaan's funeral. He had been finding it increasingly hard to sleep and had got into a bad habit of scrolling through Instagram deep into the night. As he quickly scanned through the names of those who had viewed his last Instagram story, his heart missed a beat. There, in the middle of the list, was Ishaan's name and grinning profile pic. 'It was a big shock,' he told me, when we met.

It took him only seconds to work out that it must be Ishaan's father on his son's Instagram account. Ishaan had shown his father how to log in and post photos to his account before he had gone into hospital, so that his friends could be kept updated on how he was doing. 'But just for a few seconds I thought he was alive, that it had all been a bad dream,' Amit told me ruefully. The next morning, he messaged a few of their friends and found out they had had the same reaction.

When I spoke with Amit and his friends a few months later, during a visit to his college, he told me how concerned they had all been when Ishaan died, that his social media accounts would suddenly disappear. Many of us feel the same sort of attachment to deceased social media accounts, with 59 per cent of us viewing a social media account of a friend or family member after they have died[1].

'I made screenshots of all the photos,' Amit confessed. 'Before going into hospital he was a regular poster, at least one post on either his main account or "finsta" (fake instagram account) each day, as well as countless saved stories, captions and DMs that I can't access anywhere else. I was sure the account was about to go down.'

Now, several months later, the group of friends were still unsure what was going to happen to all of Ishaan's accounts.

'I don't know if his parents are planning to leave them up, or close them down,' Amit said, 'and I don't feel I can ask them. I go and look at them sometimes...' The others in the group admitted they had done the same thing themselves; sometimes scrolling back through the photos of their holiday in Spain the previous summer; sometimes re-reading Ishaan's posts in their group chat.

'His account is like visiting a place we used to hang out,' Amit went on, putting into words how they all felt; 'we talked a lot on there, it has memories that are years old. I don't want to lose that connection, but I know it's not my decision.'

Death and dying in societies across the world, and through time, have always been accompanied by rituals that have helped those left behind deal with the loss of a loved one, celebrate that person's life, and eventually let them go. In some cultures we spend time with the body of the person who has died, to share memories and support each other. We then progress to some kind of funeral or act of celebration. Finally, we may erect a physical marker we can visit when we want to remember them. What will the digital equivalent of these rituals and conventions be?

We're entering completely uncharted territory with digital death. Options exist to 'memorialize' social media accounts, freeze them in time so they can't ever be logged into or updated, but that presents us with a very binary choice. Delete and take down a profile, or freeze it in time. Neither option may be quite right for us, or indeed what our loved one would want. Our only hope is to have more conversations about digital death among ourselves, even though we may not want to. Because Ishaan died so young, he'd never had a conversation with any of his friends or family about what he wanted to happen to all of his digital presences. It's likely that he never gave it a moment's thought.

'I'm sure his parents haven't thought about all of this,' said Amit, 'so at some point they may decide to shut them all down. We'll only find out when we try and visit them and they're not there.'

There was a brief silence in the group as they all digested how painful this would be for them.

'Would you want all his accounts left up?' I asked.

After some discussion, they agreed that Ishaan's Instagram account was the most important, mainly because of the group chat in the direct messages. One boy also said he'd listened to Ishaan's voicemail message a few times, which meant, they all now realized,

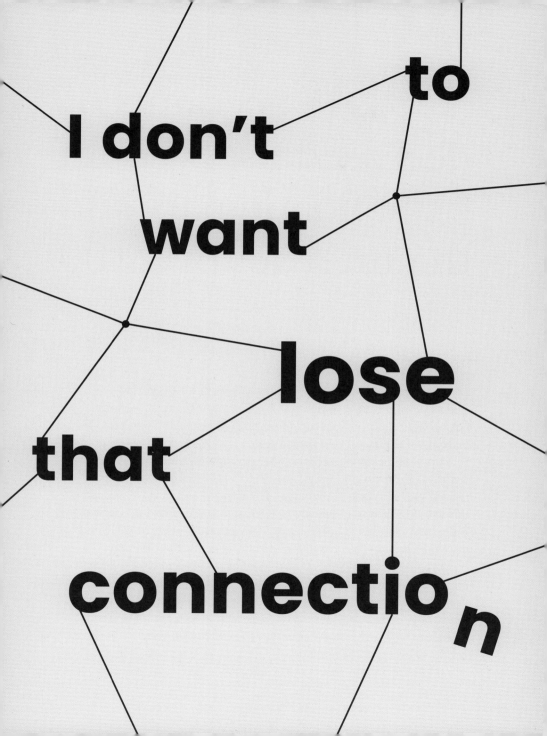

4.9bn accounts of deceased users could ⚰ be floating around the internet by 2100

his parents hadn't disconnected his phone yet. I suggested that they might want to make their own recordings of Ishaan's voicemail if they wanted to keep it, and also to save any messages he had left them on their own phones.

When we finished our chat, the group had come up with a plan. Amit was deputized to get in touch with Ishaan's dad and to raise the subject of Ishaan's accounts. The pretext was that he would be offering his help to close down any accounts the parents wanted to, but would also ask them to leave the Instagram account that they all hoped to keep up as a place to visit, to remember Ishaan.

Some people feel very superstitious thinking about what might happen after their death. You might be reading this and discovering that you're one of them. But imagine for a moment how your loved ones may feel when they're wrestling with grief after your death, while also trying to second guess what you would want them to do about all of your digital detritus. One estimate is that before the end of the century there could be 4.9 billion deceased users floating around the internet[2]. Yet, a UK survey in 2018 found that only 7 per cent of adults want their social media accounts to stay online after they die[3]. If we don't all start talking about this, we're missing an important chance to make it really clear how we feel about joining this vast collection of deceased digital presences.

'Death tech' start-up Untangle is part of a growing range of solutions being offered in the grief and loss digital space. You may shudder at the phrase 'death tech' but we're all going to have to get over our squeamishness for the sake of those we leave behind. Untangle aims to help both the bereaved and also those thinking about making helpful plans for those left behind them after they've gone. Emily Cummin, co-founder and CEO, told me, 'More and more the bereaved we help are really wrestling with this issue of what to do with the digital presences of someone they've lost.

'Start the conversation with friends and family by letting them know how you feel about your digital legacy, something which may encourage them to talk about their own,' she continues. 'You could also encourage any relatives writing or updating their wills to think about including specific instructions, or even to make a brief addition to an existing will, laying out their wishes about their social profiles and digital accounts. Ideally, they'll also document account and login details in a secure place too. The more we all talk about this, the easier it will become.'

These are the hardest conversations to have, and the newest. Make a plan and make sure someone knows about it. Your digital legacy could provide solace for some, but perpetual grief for others, so it's crucial to address this topic early. If you feel you can't think far into the future, to decide what you might want to happen when you die, or if you have absolutely no idea what you want, tell the person you most trust that they can take whatever digital decisions seem appropriate at the time. As the digital world penetrates faster and further into our lives, we may find that decisions taken about our digital legacy will be the most important legacy decisions of all.

Digital Legacies:

n. the sum of all the digital presences, accounts and assets you leave behind when you die.

⚠ SIGNS:

Social media profiles, email accounts, documents, passwords, photos, music libraries, cloud accounts, messages, websites and blogs (not an exclusive list)... these all form part of your digital legacy.

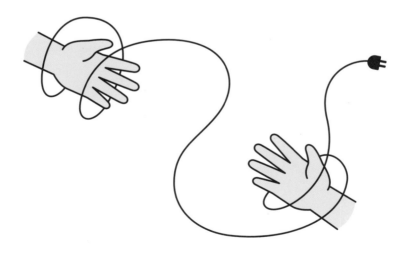

·☿· SOLUTION:

At the time of writing, Facebook will let you appoint a 'Legacy Contact' who is authorized to instruct them on memorializing or closing down your account after death. Twitter requires a copy of a death certificate to do the same. But it's not just social profiles you need to think about. Because we're all trying to be green and have opted out of paper forms of communication, more and more important documents only exist in electronic format. How can they be accessed after your death? What about family photos? If all your photos have been taken by, and reside on, your smartphone, how will they be recovered by those who might want them? Your first step should be to back these up on a hard drive to eliminate the risk of them being lost. Have you left a list of your important passwords anywhere? What about a summary of all the accounts you'd want closed? How do you want to be remembered online? If you have spent time thinking about this and have decided how you would like to be remembered, you will need to make your wishes crystal clear to your loved ones. Even if you don't put it in writing, or designate an official digital legacy executor, tell someone close to you what you would want in the event of your death.

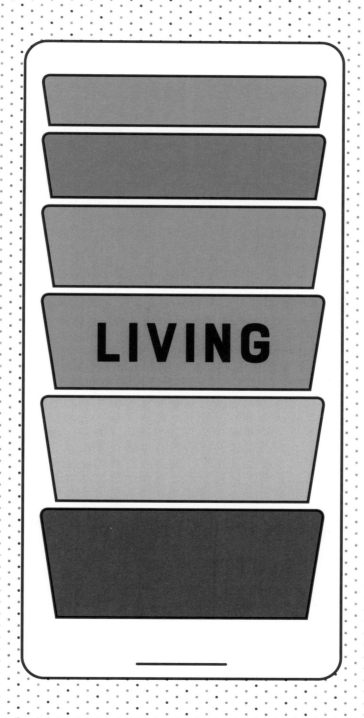

ON COMPARISON CULTURE

'Just ignore it'

The first time I spoke to a school group of 13-year-old boys, I realized that they may well be my toughest crowd, but they are also funny, cheeky and ask the best questions once you work out how to talk to them (tip: plenty of videos in very short clips). For all their bravado, they are often vulnerable and lacking in confidence. Working out how to navigate the digital world is just as intrepid and uncertain an exploration for them as it is for the rest of us.

At one particular boys' school, I was hurriedly packing away my kit after my last talk of the day, when I spied a boy out of the corner of my eye heading my way. He looked nervous.

'Can I ask you something, Miss? I liked your talk by the way,' he added hastily.

'Sure, let's talk on the way out.'

'What do you think about dumbphones?' he asked.

I had been hearing more and more about these phones. Handsets with the core functionality of a smartphone – able to make and receive calls and send texts – but with no access to the internet. In some of the workplaces I'd visited, the younger members of staff had shown me that they had switched to them. But this was the first time I'd ever had someone in a school ask me about one.

The young teen had been thinking more and more about getting one. He wanted to stay in touch with his friends but he was finding the digital world, especially social media, overwhelming. He wanted to find a way to escape but, so far, his attempts to ignore the apps on his smartphone weren't proving very successful. My talk, with its focus on how persuasive tech was designed and why it is so hard to resist, had crystallized why he was finding it tough.

I asked him what it was about the digital world that he wanted to escape from. It was the same things I always hear from teenagers: the pressure to keep up; to have an arty and creative feed; to have an exciting and full life; to keep showcasing all that over and over again online. It sounded exhausting.

This time, though, the boy (I never did get his name) also talked about body image. It was the first time I'd had that particular chat with a boy. It seemed there was a new app going around, specifically marketed at teen and pre-teen boys, which enabled a six pack to be painted on a naked torso. Everyone was uploading pictures of themselves looking like they'd been spending hours pumping iron. He knew it was all rubbish, he knew exactly what those boys actually looked like in real-life. But that didn't mean he didn't find it all depressing when he saw the images popping up in his feed.

A worrying 52 per cent of UK teens[1] now say that social media is making them feel less confident about how they look, or how interesting their life is, with one US study finding those who used Facebook the most often had poorer self-esteem, accounted for by their greater exposure to 'upward social comparisons' (viewing people who seemed to be more socially successful or attractive)[2]. Recent studies have found that those who use Facebook frequently believe that other users are happier and more successful than they are, especially when they do not know them very well offline[3].

There's more and more evidence that boys and men, having previously lagged behind women and girls, are feeling pressure in this area. It's one of the things that makes me most angry about social media; the impact it's having on young people at a time when they're most vulnerable. And the issues social media can create or exacerbate at a young age won't be left behind in childhood. They can undermine the building of solid self-esteem, secure identity and good mental health, and develop into longer term serious and life-limiting conditions. Selfie culture seems to be specifically toxic, with one study finding that frequently viewing selfies (but not group photos) posted by others, led to decreased self-esteem and decreased life satisfaction[4].

Professor David Veale, Consultant Psychiatrist and Visiting Professor at King's College in London, specializes in body dysmorphic disorder (BDD), and told me, 'Comparing is a form of ranking oneself against others to determine if they are a threat or not. Inevitably people rank the feature that is defining their "self" as less attractive than the same feature in someone else.

He wanted to the digital world

esc

52% of UK teens say social media makes them feel less confident about how they look

They therefore become more self-critical. Analysing, brooding, comparing and ranking one's features is highly toxic to one's mental health.'

There's only so many times a parent or teacher can tell a child to put their phone down and 'just ignore it' when they're scrolling on social media and finding it eating away at their self-esteem. When platforms are using persuasive tech tricks to keep kids hooked for longer and longer and serving up ads to them for apps to retouch their photos (always presented as a bit of a joke and not to be taken seriously), what chance do they have?

Luckily, our teens are getting wise to this. This boy knew tech companies weren't jumping to help him, so he had found a solution, a workaround to give him access to the digital world when he needed it, and a break when he didn't. He knew he was being played by tech and he wanted to wrest back some control.

I was encouraging about his plan. We talked as we walked out together to the car park about the merits of the dumbphones where you can use your existing smartphone SIM, so he could still keep using his smartphone occasionally if he wanted to. He hadn't realized that option existed, so he went away enthused about doing more research.

Thanks to that chat with that one boy, I've started asking teens if they know about dumbphones, and if they've ever thought about getting one. At a girls' school a while later, this time with 14-year-olds, nearly 10 per cent of the class put up their hands to say they either already had one or were thinking of swapping.

We've been advertised to, and endured attempts to manipulate our habits and ideas, for far longer than we've had smartphones. But now we simply can't escape these pocket-sized companions, we carry them around with us everywhere we go. We need to be more inventive, keep resisting, and supporting teens and young people in resisting, until better regulation of social media is introduced, and more sense is restored to the world. I'm still hopeful that it will be.

Comparison Culture:

n. the societal pressure that encourages you to constantly compare your appearance, lifestyle and achievements with others.

⚠ SIGNS:

Checking your physical appearance, career, relationship status and lifestyle against others, largely online in your social media feed. Feeling yourself inadequate or lacking by comparison. Noticing your self-esteem is negatively affected by comparing yourself with others online.

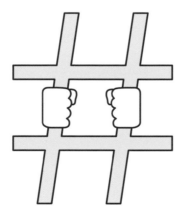

⛅ SOLUTION:

If we want to enjoy the benefits of the digital world without falling foul of the pitfalls, we need to think about ring-fencing our constant connection with it. The comparison culture on social media is a toxic mess. Although you know you're only seeing everyone's highlight reel and manipulated photos, it still makes you feel bad about your own life.

You can physically cut it out by getting a dumbphone and swearing off all social media away from your desktop, for small or large blocks of time, or permanently. Or, you can try and curate your feed so it's providing you with positive benefits. Focus on following people who post about action, not appearance. Follow far fewer people for whom you can easily make a comparison between their life and yours. Find people way outside your world, whose life isn't similar to yours in any way. Find activists, campaigners, motivational writers and artists. Your social media world is what you make it; don't let click-hungry algorithms design it for you. Take back control.

ON MULTI-SCREENING

×

'My brain has too many tabs open'

A poorly lit video appeared on Instagram stories in my feed one evening: a shot panned a darkened room from the glowing TV screen to two sofas arranged in front of it and their occupants. A voiceover, in the style of David Attenborough, whispered:

'And here we are, with huge excitement, all settling down to watch the big film...

'...and look, all five inhabitants are on their phones!'

The video did indeed show, one by one, everyone curled up on the sofas in the living room with their heads bowed over their phone screens, oblivious to the dialogue and music booming from the TV in front of them.

It's a familiar sight in our homes: 45 per cent of US adults admit they 'very often' or 'always' use another device while watching the TV (only 12 per cent say they 'never' use another device)[1]. It happens in offices, too. How many of you sit in meetings and look round the room at people tapping away on laptops, who are looking up and nodding occasionally at what's being shown on the big screen, or even sit next to those who are also checking their smartphones simultaneously?

In workplaces, clients often tell me that having two or more monitors on a desk is great for productivity and makes workers more efficient. Younger generations, the millennials and Generation Z, frequently vehemently assert that they are more than capable of being on two or more screens in any situation, without it having any impact on their focus or concentration.

If you're one of those people who still believes that 'multi-tasking' actually exists, I'm afraid you're mistaken. The whole concept of multi-tasking was born in the 1960s and was originally applied to IBM computers, coined to describe their ability to process computational tasks simultaneously. Someone got the idea that this could be applied to human brains, and that if we would all learn how to do it we'd become super-efficient. They neglected to grasp that the human brain, incredibly sophisticated though it is, is not actually a computer.

All of us are failures when it comes to multi-tasking, because as a human skill it doesn't exist. When we try to do two or more things at the same time, we spilt our focus. We take longer to do any of the things we're doing together than we would do if we were doing them separately – and we make many more mistakes. 'Continuous Partial Attention' has been coined as one phrase to describe what happens when we try and focus our attention on more than one thing continuously. It's not quite the same as multi-tasking as it seems to be motivated not by trying to be more productive, but by trying not to miss anything[2]. It definitely describes what goes on in my home most days of the week, and in yours I'm sure, too.

The belief in multi-tasking has lingered and has now spawned its evil offspring: multi-screening. This has us all believing that having several screens open all at once, all focused on different tasks, will help us speed through everything in double quick time.

Surely though, flitting between a smartphone very briefly to check notifications and messages while mainly focused on one other thing, can't really be that much of a problem? Well, yes, it is, and it's not only distracting us, it also may be making us less intelligent. A 2017 study from the University of Texas at Austin, found that the mere presence of our smartphone, even when we're not using it, can reduce our available cognitive capacity and impair our cognitive functioning, even though we believe we're giving our full attention and focus to the task at hand. So, if we can just see our smartphones nearby, our brains are automatically working less efficiently.

Away from work, where we can all see being able to focus properly might be a small advantage, when we're back at home on the sofa with our TV and smartphones, does it really matter if we're only giving each of those half of our attention? If we hear or see an ad on the radio or TV, we can instantly look this up and get more information from our smartphone or other devices – something advertisers know of course. By multi-screening, we're playing into the hands of advertisers by becoming more engaged with their ads.

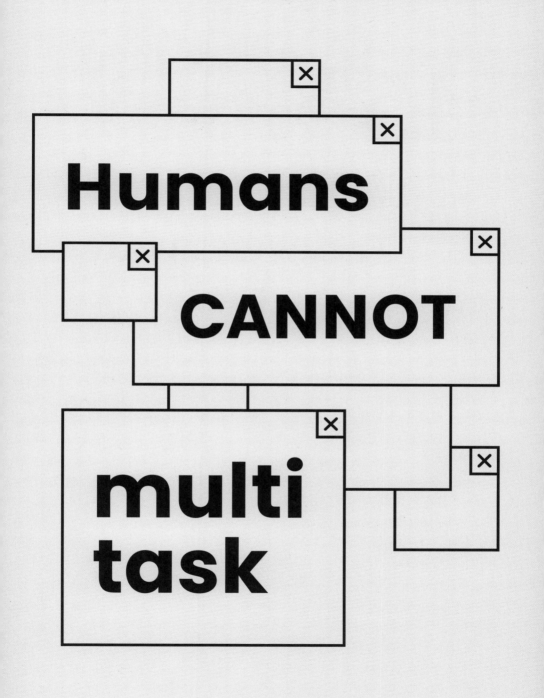

45% of US adults use another device while watching TV

Advertisers and social media companies have even tried to frame this lack of total attention as 'augmenting' or 'enhancing' our TV viewing experience. Trending hashtags encourage us all to be tweeting, posting or commenting on our TV viewing all the time, for which we definitely need two screens.

But how is it enhancing the experience? Who among us has lifted our head from our phones in the middle of a gritty crime drama and realized we have no idea what's going on? How many of us have been asked to catch up their fellow viewer on a plot development that they've missed thanks to scrolling?

More than draining our IQ, splitting our focus and reducing our productivity, our multi-screening habit is robbing us of the experience of being really fully present in anything we are doing. We're no longer able to be completely immersed in a drama, a concert or even a piece of work, reducing the chances we may be moved, brought joy or even feel the satisfaction of a job well done. Being able to concentrate on one thing brings us less stress and more enjoyment.

Make a mindful and active choice to 'single screen' at times, and for tasks that are important to you. Is that when you're viewing TV in the evening with the family? Is it at work when you're focused on a tricky but important project? Maybe it's when you settle down on your own to immerse yourself in that drama or documentary you've been saving for yourself? Whenever or wherever it is, set your own rules, but carve out some regular time to allow yourself to be fully absorbed with just one screen.

We're all rushing to learn meditation, downloading mindfulness apps, finding time for yoga. Be. More. Present. All we need to do is fully focus on one thing at a time. Even if that's the watching of a low-brow, thoroughly enjoyable film on the television with our family.

Choose a screen to pick a lane: focus and success, or distraction and stress.

Multi-Screening:

v. the use of multiple digital devices at the same time, for example mobile phones and the television.

⚠ SIGNS:

You look around you and in your sightline is more than one screen, on and ready for use. You always have your smartphone in your hand while watching TV. Your smartphone is out on your desk at work while you're on your desktop or laptop. You use your laptop in meetings, presentations, seminars and lectures. You scroll on your smartphone in the cinema.

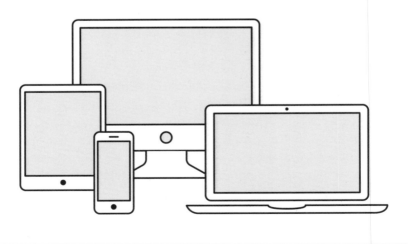

⌁ SOLUTION:

Are you someone that taps at a laptop in meetings, while glancing at the PowerPoint on the big screen? Stop it. Don't take phones into meetings either. Assess your working practices to see if you need to make changes to reduce multi-tasking. If you're the boss, lead by example and safeguard your employees and colleagues from multi-screening. Look at the options for cutting down on multiple desktop monitors, instigate One Screen meetings and have a conversation about multi-tasking and split focus in the workplace so everyone understands the science. Watch productivity improve as you limit multi-screen use in your workplace and help those around you find their focus again. At home, implement a ban on smartphones in front of the television. If this feels too extreme, or you fear your family will resist, perhaps try a gradual approach of reducing the time spent on multiple screens, or at least ringfence certain days, hours or types of viewing when they are put away. Remind yourself that your brain is not a computer. It can, and will, become overloaded and lose focus if you attempt too much at once. Do one thing at a time.

ON GAMING ADDICTION

—

'He's thrown
everything away'

I love chatting to Uber drivers. I've had some amazing conversations about where they come from, their daily lives, and what's really going on in the city they drive through every day. There is one conversation that has always stuck in my head.

The driver had picked me up from a school talk in North London and was doing an incredible job of weaving through the backstreets, avoiding the snarled-up traffic to get me home.

'I used to drive this way every day, dropping my son off at school,' he explained. Radiating pride, he explained that his son had won a full academic scholarship to a top boys' school in London. His son had been the first member of the family to get such a priceless opportunity, since the father had arrived in the UK with his own parents from Sri Lanka a few decades ago. Every weekday he had driven his son the two-hour journey from their home to get him to school, then picked him up every day afterwards.

When he had left the school, the son had secured a place at Imperial College London to study maths. I could hear in the father's voice how in awe he was of him.

'But now he spends all day in his room,' he told me. 'I can't get him out, he's thrown everything away.'

The son had started playing computer games at school and his father had initially encouraged him, thinking that it was helping with his maths and computer science studies. It didn't affect his studies to begin with but when he went to university and was in charge of his own time, all that changed. The father gradually realized that his son was missing lectures, avoiding any student social activities and was spending all hours huddled alone in his room playing computer games. Eventually, the high-performing apple of his eye had failed his first-year exams and had dropped out of university altogether. He had arrived back home, games consoles in hand, to remain permanently closeted in his childhood bedroom.

'He doesn't look happy,' he told me, his shoulders hunching more tightly over the steering wheel as he talked. 'He's not washing, hardly eating, and when I question all the game playing, he gets angry and tells me it's the only thing that makes him happy. He says I'm too old to get what gaming is all about.'

I've had many conversations like this over the last decade, but this was the one that stood out. It was the raw emotion in the father's voice that I remember so vividly.

Lots of people find video gaming a very positive experience for them. I had a chat recently with a couple of men in their early 30s who told me how their multi-player games had been a lifeline through the lockdown enforced by the coronavirus pandemic. Playing had made them feel connected with their mates, who they probably wouldn't have reached out to in any other way. Unable to go to the pub, they jumped on the game and everyone would ask how they were and how their day was. It was like having a support group, they said, because they were on the same team playing the same game.

Gaming can have positive effects despite the negative stigma, and in the above case added to those young men's lives. But for the driver's son, it was having devastating consequences. It may be that he was simply more susceptible to the addictive features of computer gaming in the first place. A study in 2005 found that dopamine (a feel-good chemical in the brain) levels doubled when people were playing video games. Only about 10 per cent of the adult population will ever become addicted to any substance, or process, at any point in their lives, but for those who do, video game addiction is a real risk. More than 2 billion people play video games globally[1], with 77 per cent of all US men aged 18 to 29 playing them[2] (the average age of a gamer is 35[3]), so this is not a minority interest.

The World Health Organization (WHO) formally added Gaming Disorder (also called 'digital-gaming' or 'video-gaming') to its International Classification of Diseases in 2018, with estimates that 0.3–1 per cent of the population may qualify for an acute diagnosis of gaming disorder[4]. To qualify for a diagnosis the key criteria is that time spent on gaming is seen to be escalating and taking priority over other daily activities with a real disregard for the negative consequences – 'My life is falling apart but I don't care',

HIS LIFE WAS BECOMING SMALLER AND SMALLER

for example. With impulse control not fully developing until around the age of 25, it's the youngest gamers who can be more susceptible to it. This is exasperated by the increasing prevalence of virtual bundles of random in-game items (such as weapons or costumes) exchanged for real-world money, known as 'loot boxes', despite concerns of children being exposed to gambling at an early age. Research by the University of York indicates that from 2010–2019, the presence of loot boxes has increased from around 4 per cent to 71 per cent[5].

China was the first country to label online addiction a disorder in 2008, and their 'internet boot camps' for young people, specializing in a mixture of therapy and military-style treatment, have been widely publicized ever since an eye-opening *New York*

From 2010 to 2019, the presence of loot boxes in major games increased from 4% to 71%

Times documentary featured them in 2014[6]. In the documentary, Tao Ran, Director of the Daxing Center, said, 'Some kids are so hooked on these games they think taking a restroom break will affect their performance at the games. So, they wear a diaper.'

How can we tell if gaming has turned from a passion into a problem? Or is heading that way? Dr Richard Graham is a Consultant Child and Adolescent Psychiatrist who established the first Technology Addiction Service for Young People in the UK in 2010 and who contributed to the WHO's consideration of Gaming Disorder as a medical diagnosis. 'We try and work out whether your child continues to game when their friends know it is time to stop,' he says. 'As with other addictions, the person who carries on when others have stopped might have a problem controlling their use. Every person who struggles with an addiction has a back story, and gaming may be something that helps them escape or avoid a problem somewhere else (e.g. at school); if you know that you may focus help where it is most needed.'

I gave the details of a tech addiction clinic to the Uber driver and I urged him to contact them and get some guidance, even if his son wouldn't contact them himself. I reassured him that he was absolutely right to be worried, and to ignore the jibes that he was out of touch. If you're not immersed in the digital or gaming world, it's easy to be put off by deflections that you're a digital dinosaur. But the father's instincts that his son was struggling were right.

I've had one half of a couple tell me their partner is gaming so much they hardly talk any more. I've had roommates tell me about the one who stays up late in their room gaming for hours, missing work the next day and losing their job. I've had parents tell me about a child glued to a games console, no longer taking part in a sport they used to love. In all these cases the issue is the same: it's what's being given up in order to devote hours to gaming that is evidence of a problem. If your loved one isn't listening to the argument that their relentless gaming is bad for them, try filling them in on all the research that shows the longer someone spends sitting in front of a screen in their life, the shorter and less healthy that life will be.

If you see deeply worrying behaviour in anyone you love, glued to a games console and neglecting everything else in their life, don't let them tell you that you don't understand because you're not a gamer. Problem signs can be clear withdrawal symptoms, deceiving family and friends about their gaming habits, reliance on gaming to relieve a negative mood, and loss of interest in previous hobbies. If you notice any of these, try and set time limits for play, keep consoles and other devices out of their room so they can't play well into the night and encourage other activities like physical exercise. If problems persist, push them to get some professional help.

Gaming Addiction [aka 'gaming disorder']:

n. addiction to computer games, impaired control over gaming.

⚠ SIGNS:

Giving increasing time to gaming to the extent that gaming takes precedence over your other interests and daily activities. Continuation or escalation of gaming despite the negative consequences. Thinking about gaming all of the time. Feeling bad when you can't play. Not being able to stop gaming, even though you want to. All this going on for a period of longer than 12 months.

💡 SOLUTION:

Get help from a doctor or therapist as soon as you think gaming is getting out of hand. It may be that gaming addiction is the problem, or it may be masking another mental health issue such as depression or anxiety. If you're helping someone else, set limits for their gaming and enforce them. Remove games consoles from the bedroom so that playing into the night is not possible. Design a structure for the day that involves getting exercise, getting outside and eating and sleeping properly. Like many other addictions to processes rather than substances, video games take up a lot of time and stopping altogether may leave a huge void in your, or someone else's, life which can cause relapses. Start by curtailing how much time is spent gaming; make gaming a part of the day – not the whole of it. Incorporate set breaks at least every hour and perhaps try games that encourage physical activity and family participation.

ON TROLLING

—

'No one wants to
listen to you'

Don't feed the trolls.

This is arguably the first rule of Twitter if you want to survive it. But what if they strike first?

Amna had just finished talking on a morning radio show that she'd been invited on to discuss the work of her research laboratory. She formed part of a group of specialist medical researchers carrying out fairly uncontentious work. Whenever she mentioned the field of study she worked in outside the lab, she was usually met with only vague polite interest. She wasn't usually the media spokesperson, but she'd been happy to go on and chat about their work. She was relieved it all seemed to have gone without a hitch, and she hoped she'd done a good job of explaining the complexities of their research to the listeners.

'My phone started buzzing off the hook the minute I switched it back on,' she said. 'There were some lovely messages from friends and family saying that they'd heard me and thought I'd explained the research really well. There was also one that warned me not to engage "with those idiots" on Twitter. I couldn't help myself, I had to look.'

'No one wants to listen to you,' read one tweet.

*'Attention-seeking b****,'* was another.

There were others, too unpleasant to list.

'I was horrified,' she said. 'I clicked on the names of the accounts that had tweeted to find out who they were, but none of them had any faces on their profile pics and they all had weird names. I was standing there playing back in my head everything I had said in the interview to work out what might have come across as "attention-seeking". I couldn't think of anything. I just didn't know what had prompted the attack. Some of the messages scared me.'

Of course, Amna had done absolutely nothing wrong. It was her first experience of being attacked online, something unfortunately millions of people experience every day. In 2017, 1 per cent of UK internet users (an estimated 620,000 people[1]) reported they had been trolled online at least once over the previous 12 months[2].

For 16–24-year-olds this went up to 5 per cent, or 3 million users. Trolling appears most on social media: 38 per cent of US internet users say they see trolling on social platforms, while 23 per cent have seen it on video sharing websites[3].

While many trolls are individuals dedicated to abusive online behaviour, either because of sociopathic tendencies or because they are targeting and attacking specific groups (like the misogynistic online communities Laura Bates uncovered in her book *Men who Hate Women*), one area of trolling which has been rather overlooked is the extent to which we may all be guilty of online attacks ourselves.

Something seems to happen to our self-restraint when we are online. We lose it. We say (type) things we would never dream of saying when we are face-to-face with anyone. It's not just about being anonymous, though many people hide behind fake profiles in order to make attacks on others. Many more people make absolutely no attempt to hide their identities, yet aggressively attack and insult others in a way that would surprise you if you met them in person. Although only 45 per cent of US adults in 2014 had heard the term 'troll' and knew what it meant, 28 per cent admitted they had carried out malicious online attacks against someone they didn't know. And 23 per cent said they had also 'maliciously argued over an opinion with a stranger'[4]. It has also become too glib to dismiss all trolling just as the type which is part of organized and funded attacks online with a political agenda (see 'Fake News', page 30); I'm drawing a clear line here between that kind of activity and individuals trolling each other. If 1 in 4 adults have admitted to doing this when asked, think for a minute of all those who didn't hold their hand up. You, or someone you know, has almost certainly engaged in this kind of behaviour at one time or another online.

We need to all look at what we can do to reduce this kind of behaviour, even if we're not trying to intentionally troll. Before hitting that send button, put yourself in the recipient's shoes and

WE LOSE OUR SELF-RESTRAINT

28% of US adults admit they have carried out malicious attacks !!! online

consider their feelings; remember that there is a person behind the avatar and handle. How do you think your comments will make them feel? Be kind and consider whether you'd find it acceptable to say these things if you were face to face with them. If you're feeling angry about something, perhaps take a break and try to calm down before responding or messaging. Precious few issues are resolved in online arguments. Step away from rows when you see them escalating – conflict fades away if no one is piling in.

Where more dedicated trolling is concerned, the digital world with its lack of regulation, and the tech giants' reluctance to properly police content on their platforms, has given trolls full licence to let rip. Governments have been shockingly slow to propose regulation to deal with this. At the time of writing, in the UK the Online Harms Bill[5], first proposed in 2019, was still making its torturous way through the parliamentary process. Perhaps the unforgivably slow pace of introducing regulation has been because those most often attacked are not highly represented by those seated in parliament? Although MPs and politicians are among the most trolled, it's often women and minority groups that bear the brunt of online abuse. Nineteen female MPs stood down ahead of the snap general election in the UK in December 2019 with at least four out of the nineteen explicitly citing online intimidation and harassment as one of the reasons they no longer felt able to continue in politics.

The targeting of members of minority groups is further evidenced in the 'Troll Report' by Amnesty International, which in 2017 found that women are 27 times more likely to be victims of online trolling and abuse than men[6]. Nearly a quarter (23 per cent) of the women surveyed across eight countries said they had experienced online abuse or harassment at least once, ranging from 16 per cent in Italy to 33 per cent in the US[7]. Over half (59 per cent) of women who experienced abuse online said it came from complete strangers[8]. Ethnic minorities and members of the LGBTQI community are also often in the firing line, with black women disproportionately targeted. The same Amnesty International report found black women were an incredible 84 per cent more likely than white women to be mentioned in abusive or problematic tweets[9]. The lazy defence of trolling has been that it's just free speech in action. But if large swathes of society are effectively silenced and are targeted online, then it's clear this is anything but free speech if only certain people are allowed to speak freely.

If you're reading this and you've never been attacked in any way online, you're lucky. Someone close to you has almost certainly experienced this though, and they need your support and help. Reach out to those around you who are especially active on social media and ask them if they have unpleasant experiences of online attacks. We read trolls' comments in our heads and silently internalize them, so being able to speak to someone openly about how reading these makes them feel can help them mentally move on from the situation. Dedicated trolls thrive on reactions, so tell anyone who is suffering to make sure they're not engaged with and to quickly block or report accounts.

I couldn't undo the tweets for Amna, and I couldn't make her easily forget them. But I could listen. And I could reassure her that it was nothing to do with her and help her see that the problem lay with the people tweeting. I shared with her my own experiences and I empathized with how unpleasant it is, and how unsettling it can be. Most of all I urged her not to delete her accounts, to keeping discussing her work online and contributing to debates. I wanted her to draw a very clear line between engaging in debate when a challenge was genuinely coming from a place of misunderstanding, questioning further or asking her to clarify her position. If an attack was personal and intended to be demeaning and offensive, I told her to simply not engage.

I can't sugar-coat it: trolling and abuse is one of the most toxic internet issues right now. But if it hasn't happened to you, don't think this is someone else's problem. It has devastating effects on people's mental health, discourages debate and leads to only the anonymous trolls having the luxury of free speech. This is a problem for all of us. If we want to keep our digital spaces safe, we need to stop engaging in this behaviour ourselves, and support others and report trolling when we see it happening. We need to reach out to those being targeted and speak to them so that they're not internalizing the abuse on their own. And we must keep up the pressure for legislation and regulation in our digital communities. The Online Harms Bill must pass in the UK and be given real teeth to act against trolling. Similar bills must be passed internationally. Financial penalties against platforms for failing to act must be hefty and imposed with no wiggle room. Let's clean up our online town squares and make them safe spaces for debate and (civil) disagreements. It's beyond time for the digital sheriff to come to town.

Trolling:

v. deliberately targeting individuals online in chat rooms, message boards and forums, social media and other platforms by posting inflammatory and offensive messages, with the intent of provoking a reaction.

⚠ SIGNS:

Often associated with anonymous or faceless accounts, trolling might be recognized for its incendiary comments and its clear intention to disrupt and spread hate, perhaps as a provocative response or as a tool to silence other internet users and discourage them from getting involved in online discussion.

☀ SOLUTION:

My three-step strategy for trolls is: Report, Block, Support. Reporting used to be problematic on social media platforms but they are getting much better at providing tools and routes to do that now. **Report** any persistent harassers after three strikes and anyone who posts abuse or threats immediately. **Block** users from being able to contact or message you again. Remember to do this after you have reported them, so you can provide links and names to the moderators of the site. Delete any messages that may remain in any format that you can still see. There's no point beating yourself up by reading nasty messages over and over again. If you notice someone being harassed or targeted online, do what you would do if you spotted it happening in public. Go over and offer them **support**. Send a private message saying you can see what's going on and suggest what they can do. A public message calling it out is even better.

Remember what Edmund Burke said: 'The only thing necessary for the triumph of evil is for good men* to do nothing.' Trolls won't go away unless we shine a light into all their dark places. We also need to be personally accountable and ensure we think before we speak or send a message to someone on social media; take a step back and remember that behind the avatar is a real person with real feelings. It's going to take all of us.

*all genders included.

ON VAMPIRE SHOPPERS

———

'It doesn't feel like
real money'

Marianne was interviewing me for a magazine feature on adopting healthy new tech habits for the New Year. But I was beginning to get the distinct impression she was using the interview as an excuse to get help with some of her own issues.

'Do you think too much online shopping can be a problem? Like, buying loads of things you don't really need because it's so easy to do?' she asked, in a pause in the interview.

'Is this you?' I hazarded a guess.

She laughed, 'My husband says I have a real problem. There's a constant stream of parcels and bags coming to the house. If I'm up late for a deadline I'll distract myself by scrolling on my phone. Then there'll be an advert for something that catches my eye. I find myself compulsively clicking and adding stuff to my basket without a second thought. Before I know it, I've spent a hundred pounds on something I'm later not even sure I want. And of course, I never return most of it.'

Marianne confessed that the scale of her purchases were getting bigger too – from a discounted jacket to a full-price sofa, the price tag was becoming less of an obstacle when it came to the speed of the purchase. She was visibly relieved when I told her that she was not alone. In fact, late-night impulse shoppers like her are increasingly targeted by online retailers as they are so lucrative. Nocturnal shoppers apparently spend 20 per cent more than shoppers browsing during the day[1]. They even have a name – 'vampire shoppers' – to reflect the fact that they come out late at night (and maybe also because they drain the life blood out of the victim's bank account).

It's a habit that is on the rise. Barclaycard has reported that one in three shoppers now spend more money online at night than during the day, compared to 5 years ago[2]. And when winter comes and nights get longer we spend even more. In winter months, shoppers spend on average 2 hours 12 minutes browsing after dark, compared to 1 hour 30 minutes in the summer. In fact, 10.18pm was cited in one piece of research as the peak time for spending, with one in fifteen of all purchases online in the UK made between midnight and 6am[3].

I asked Marianne if she thought her late-night online shopping was getting any worse, and whether anything in particular was triggering it. Apple Pay being introduced onto the iPhone in 2014 was when things had escalated for her. There is no need to stop and fill in your card details any more or fill in a form. There is also no time for you to pause and hesitate thanks to this shortened shopping journey. Instant gratification was inevitably followed by buyer's remorse and growing debt.

This is precisely why one-click features have been so successful for online retailers. The incredible speed of buying online creates the perfect environment for impulse buying, the highly lucrative area where retailers make so much of their money. Ethical consumerism asks of all of us that we think before we buy, that we are mindful consumers – 'mindsumerism' has been coined as a neat term for this – instead of mindlessly moving from one purchase to the next. Being concerned about sustainability and the impact of our hyper-consumerism on the planet also requires that we all stop and question our shopping habits. The fevered world of one-click shopping severely hampers all our chances of doing any of this.

Eliminating the breathing space to rein in our self-destructive impulses is one of the most dangerous features of the digital world. It impacts so much of what we do, from firing off an angry text without stopping to calm down, to mindlessly adding items to our online baskets when we're tired, or in need of the boost we think shopping will give us.

'The problem is it just doesn't feel like real money,' Marianne continued. 'It's not like handing over a debit card in a shop. It's just a click. It feels exactly the same as clicking a "like" button. It only hits me that I've actually spent anything when I see the damage to my account balance and panic.'

Marianne's habits were starting to feel akin to gambling, as she played with shopping online, trivializing the impact on her finances and finding herself with bags and boxes of items she'd never wear, and never return for refunds. 'Click and regret' has all

JUST ONE CLICK...

of us wasting over half a billion pounds online every year in the UK alone, buying things we realize we actually don't want when they arrive at our doors. Around 27 per cent of UK adults say they order goods online, which they then regret but fail to return, wasting about £52 per person every year[4].

For Marianne, Pinterest was often a trigger. She would find herself browsing beautiful boards of home interiors before clicking through to buy their featured products. Instagram was also a problem: the 'swipe up' feature on stylish influencers' stories made it very easy for her to get carried away buying the clothes and products they were promoting.

There were a few things that helped to create the ideal conditions for Marianne's online shopping to get out of control. Having her phone in the bedroom in the first place was definitely not helping, but as a journalist she often had to be on call, so that wasn't likely

Nocturnal online shoppers spend 20% more than daytime shoppers

to change. Easy access to payment methods was something she could look at though. So, she agreed as we chatted further, that she was going to remove all her linked credit cards from Apple Pay and just have her bank debit card connected. She was going to do the same on Amazon, and she was going to make sure her browser wasn't storing any credit cards to use via the auto-fill feature.

My last suggestion was one I'd made to other late-night shoppers, often with great success: 'Next time you get the urge to buy something, I want you to experiment with adding things to your online basket as usual but then leaving them in there overnight. If you're online shopping around 1am,' which Marianne had said was the time she usually found herself buying, 'it's unlikely that what catches your eye will have sold out by 8am the next morning. Leave it in the basket, tell yourself you'll complete the purchase the next day if you still want it. Then log off and go to sleep.'

This simple tactic is surprisingly effective. Browsing and adding items to shopping baskets still gives you the buzz of shopping, but sleeping on it often saves you from spending your credit unwisely. Pleasure without the pain. In the cold light of day you'll realize that you really didn't need another kitchen gadget, cushion cover or plant holder, however much of a bargain they had seemed the night before.

The introduction of one-click shopping really changed the game for retailers online. Abandoned items in online shopping baskets was ecommerce's biggest headache. 'Have you forgotten something?' emails have some success. But making sure it's hassle-free to complete the purchase in the first place is what's made the difference. Combine that ease with the soaring hours we are all spending online and the result has been dwindling bank accounts for many of us. There's no time of day or night when we can't be sold to.

Over-spending has been linked as a habit to poor mental health[5], and it's not hard to see how the spend, spend, spend online shopping environment can conspire to make even the most robust of us succumb. Though online gambling, which also preys on the vulnerable, is regulated, online shopping and the tricks used to lure purchasers into spending more than they intended to, is not. Governments are not exactly queuing up to regulate this part of the economy, which brings so much cash into their national tax coffers. We must be wary of the tricks that cause us to be trigger-happy in our nocturnal spending and protect ourselves, and others, while no one else is doing it for us.

If late-night shopping is convenient and useful for you, keep doing it. But it's important to acknowledge the fact that by moving to a more cashless economy, we need to scrutinize our financial behaviours more intently. Take a step back and ask yourself: would you go shopping at 1am on the high-street? How does the thought of you handing over your hard-earned, physical cash to a shopkeeper for the item make you feel? It's time to take a more considered approach when shopping online. Your bank account will tell you if you have the balance right.

Vampire Shopping:

v. online shopping late at night, usually between 1am and 4am, aka 'zombie hour purchasers'.

⚠ SIGNS:

Online shopping largely from your bed late at night while scrolling on your phone or other digital device. Making more purchases after dark than at any other time.

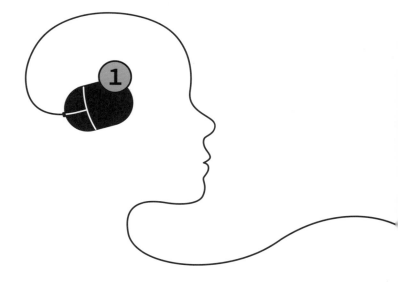

💡 SOLUTION:

The first step would be to analyse your spending habits. If you can see that most of your online shopping happens at nighttime, it would be worthwhile taking steps to limit your spending abilities during this time. Unlink credit cards from one-click features to make it harder to shop online. Don't use auto-fill (a dangerous feature for data security anyway) – go through your saved information on your devices and remove any information, including bank cards, that you have previously saved. This will add valuable extra steps to the process of online shopping, giving you time to reflect and think on your proposed purchases before clicking the buy now button.

Put items in the shopping basket and don't buy until the next morning. Use the HALT acronym when online shopping (Am I 'Hungry, Angry, Lonely or Tired'?) to question your impulse to shop. If any of these states apply to how you are currently feeling, your judgement may be impaired, so it would be wise to delay shopping until those feelings have passed. Use website blockers and apps to limit access to specific websites on your phone late at night and fight the impulse to ignore the settings you've put in place. It may take some perseverance and willpower. Unsubscribe from retailer mailing lists. If you can, leave your phone outside your bedroom at night to limit the amount of time you spend with it, specifically during those dangerous nighttime hours when you are prone to spending unnecessarily.

ON THE QUANTIFIED SELF

'It's dominating
our lives'

E very night as Michael and Sinead settle down for their evening in front of the TV, the same routine begins.

The minute an ad break starts, Michael leaps to his feet and starts marching briskly between the living room and the kitchen in an infinite loop. Keeping a close eye on his smartwatch, his routine doesn't falter until the step counter hits his 10,000 daily step target.

'Sometimes he runs up and down the stairs, if he has a lot of steps to make up,' Sinead told me, 'but usually he just marches in a really irritating loop between the two rooms. It was impossible during lockdown, when we were stuck at home. He saw he was getting in fewer steps during the day, so panicked and went into overdrive. The kids and I had to give up and eat dinner without him in the end.'

But the habit that's really starting to get on Sinead's nerves is Michael's obsession with his sleep tracker.

'There was absolutely nothing wrong with his sleep before,' she told me in exasperation, 'he's always just hit the mattress and fallen fast asleep. But ever since he got this sleep tracker, he's become obsessive about how many hours he gets. Now he's sleeping really badly. I'm sure he only wakes up in the night because he's worrying about what he's going to find on the tracker in the morning. I'm moving into the spare room if it goes on much longer. All his tracking and measuring is completely dominating our lives.'

Measuring his physical activity and his sleep seems like a very healthy thing for Michael to be doing, right? With all the headlines about the obesity crisis, and how sedentary we've all become, surely we should all be applauding his attention to the health targets he's set himself?

Well, up to a point.

Measuring ourselves and setting targets for our activity is not a new phenomenon. At school we were probably given targets in physical education for the time it should take us to run a certain distance, or the length we should be able to jump. Later, as we moved through our working lives, we might have tried to fit in three exercise classes a week, vaguely aware that we should be doing about that number. Or, we might have tried to clock up eight hours of sleep a night, because we'd seen that duration being mentioned a few times as being healthy.

But the explosion of wearable fitness and health trackers brings with it the danger of transforming the benign habit of keeping an eye on our bodies into an obsession. By 2019, one in five Americans had a smartwatch or fitness tracker[1], with nearly one-third of regular wearable tech users saying they felt 'naked' without their device on[2]. We're fixating on measuring and quantity in all areas of our lives now because it's easy to measure, neglecting quality, because it isn't. It seems like there's nothing we can't measure about our bodies – the number of kilograms we weigh, the litres of water we drink, the calories we consume, the steps we take every day, the hours we sleep every night. Sophisticated weighing scales, which only existed in gyms or medical environments a decade ago, will now let us measure our muscle mass, body water content and bone density at home. During the pandemic there was a rush to buy fingertip oxygen altimeters to measure our blood oxygen. We're turning our homes into mini-labs and drowning under data, without being gifted with the skills to meaningfully interpret what they all mean, and what we need as a result.

Take those 10,000 steps that Michael has set himself. The idea that it's the ideal number comes from no more scientific a source than a Japanese marketing campaign. Around the 1964 Tokyo Olympics, a pedometer with a catchy name was launched – Manpo-kei: 'man' for 10,000, 'po' for steps and 'kei' for meter. It was a hugely successful campaign, and 10,000 stuck in everyone's heads as the perfect number to aim for.

As for sleep, even sleep experts acknowledge that what constitutes a 'good' night's sleep can vary hugely between individuals depending on their genetic make-up, their age and even their job. And it probably can't be reduced down to a specific number of hours. More important, what's conducive to a good night's sleep

Perfection can push us to breaking point

is to be fully relaxed, not worrying about the exact position of a sleep tracker under the mattress and whether it's picking up every movement. Sleep trackers may even make the thing we're trying to track, sleep quality, much worse.

Guy Leschziner, professor of neurology and sleep medicine at Guys' and St Thomas' Hospitals and King's College London, tells me:

'The use of tracking technology has a certain logic to it. If a tracker is telling you that you have not done enough exercise, or your blood pressure is too high, these are all things you can actively influence. You can get up off the sofa, exercise more, or even go to the doctor for medication. The problem with sleep is that, if you have difficulty sleeping, no tracker confirming your poor sleep will help you. In fact, quite the opposite. Confirmation of your lack of sleep will increase your anxiety around your sleep further, potentially making your sleep even worse than it was. If you combine that with the reality that sleep trackers are generally inaccurate, especially for those people with insomnia, it can create a particularly toxic environment for sleep.'

Those who produce and market activity trackers use similar techniques to social media companies to get us hooked on them. Activity trackers send us urgent push notifications when we're falling short, and then reward us with buzzes when we've achieved our goal. Buzzes that produce little dopamine bursts of pleasure in our brains. If our lives feel out of control, fixating on our step count, or the length of our sleep, may give us the illusion of being on top of something important. But if we focus on counting instead of experiencing, we're missing out.

Merely counting can morph into inflexibility, as it was in danger of doing with Michael. Enthusiasm for an activity that might improve our health may change from something our families gently tease us about, to obsessive behaviour and even an addiction.

We can track calories or weight loss, for example, to the point where eating becomes disordered and a serious mental health issue develops. One study in Singapore showed 26.1 per cent of participants said that fitness/exercise/weight loss apps had further perpetuated their disordered eating behaviours. In addition, the study showed that any calorie counting smartphone app usage was found to be associated with younger age and greater eating disorder prevalence[3]. Another study looking at the effects of calorie-counting applications on US college students, found that those who identified with regular calorie tracking on a smart phone app actually endorsed disordered eating[4].

Quantifying everything we do reduces us to nothing more than dots and lines on a graph. In trying to improve our life we find we have reduced it to a set of boxes we must tick daily. Marking our day as a success because we've hit our step count tells us nothing about our experience of it. Walking around and around our homes at night has nowhere like the same health benefit as a walk outside in nature in the middle of the day. Spending just 20 minutes in a park or green space every day, even if you don't exercise, has been associated with a 64 per cent overall improvement in life satisfaction[5]. Is hitting that mythical 10,000 steps a day delivering the same? The drive for perfection can push us to breaking point as we dementedly try to hit our targets and goals for the day, ignoring those around us. If all that counting is causing you to miss out on life, as Michael's was, you're counting the wrong things.

I told Sinead to go home and stage a family intervention by hiding all of Michael's gadgets in a drawer for a week (I actually told her to throw them in the bin, but she felt that might be a step too far), and to tell him to stop measuring, and to start living.

The Quantified Self:

n. the phenomenon of self-tracking every element of our lives with technology, aka 'lifelogging'.

⚠ SIGNS:

Using fitness trackers, apps and gadgets to measure and record daily life, with the goal of improving physical and mental performance and overall wellbeing.

☀ SOLUTION:

By all means use fitness and health trackers but keep an eye out for obsessional tendencies. Try and develop the habit of tracking and then becoming a neutral observer, rather than associating a positive or negative judgement with your results: 'Oh, I've walked 5,000 steps today, that's interesting.' Observe and don't comment or judge. Take breaks and have whole days off tracking. Do not panic about breaking a tracking 'streak'. The more panicked you feel at the thought of time without tracking, the more you probably need the break.

Remember that you should be seeking out quality as well as quantity in all aspects of your life. If tracking is taking up more of your attention than simply living; if you feel 'naked' without your wearable tech; or if you have become a slave to your tracker – answering to its every demand and religiously checking its data, drowning in graphs, charts and statistics – throw them out. If throwing them out, going cold turkey, seems like an impossible task, perhaps try limiting your use of them to certain times in the day or for certain activities only, rather than tracking your entire day?

ON SMOMBIES

—

'*@%&!'

I saw him before he saw me. But, more unfortunately, before he saw the lamppost.

'*@%&!'

Head down, peering at something indecipherable on the tiny screen in his hand, the 20-something man walking towards me had just smacked his face right into the lamppost.

Rubbing his forehead and nose in a bit of a daze, this 'smombie' (or smartphone zombie) shot an embarrassed sideways glance at me as I came level with him, then hurried off down the side road, to avoid the humiliation of me expressing any concern.

This isn't a slapstick movie scene or good material for a funny anecdote; this is part of an increasingly serious issue. Smartphones are called 'weapons of mass distraction' for a very good reason. Once, I saw a young woman fall off the pavement as she chatted on her phone, misjudging her steps and tumbling right into the road.

Both those two escaped any harm, but serious injuries or deaths by what's now called 'distracted walking' are on the rise everywhere in the world, running into thousands globally every year, as pedestrians increasingly step straight out into traffic while talking or texting on their phones. The numbers for this are relatively low, but they're growing at a rate that suggests it's becoming a real issue. A 2013 US study found distracted walking injuries were rising year-on-year, with 1,506 recorded in US emergency rooms in 2010, up from 256 in 2005[1]. The 21–25 age group were especially likely to be involved.

It's impacting city planning, inspiring expensive precautionary measures and heavy fines, yet numbers of smombie injuries still rise each year, because when we're walking while peering down at our smartphones, we really are almost totally oblivious, and blind, to what's going on around us. Research in 2014 by Japanese mobile company NTT Domoco, estimated that the field of vision of the average smartphone-peering pedestrian is a tiny 5 per cent of their non-smartphone-wielding counterpart. They ran a computer simulation to see what would happen if 1,500 pedestrians attempted to cross Tokyo's hectic Shibuya crossing while looking at their smartphones. Their results showed only one-third would make it across without mishap; the rest suffered with 446 collisions, 103 knockdowns and 21 dropped phones – yes, that means 82 of the 103 knockdowns managed to hit the ground still clutching on to their smartphones…

Distracted driving, usually involving texting on a smartphone at the wheel of a car, is subject to laws banning it in most countries of the world. But distracted walking is proving to be just as dangerous. In the US in 2016 there were 6,000 pedestrian deaths, the highest number in more than 20 years, with mobile phone use by pedestrians cited as one of the major factors for the rise[2]. It's such a concern that at least ten US states have debated legislation to make it illegal (according to the National Conference of State Legislatures) but it's only been passed into law at city level so far in two: Rexburgh, Idaho and Honolulu, Hawaii.

It's the combination of FOMO (Fear of Missing Out), our over-reliance on Google Maps, and how distracting our smartphones are, that makes it so hard for us to put them down while walking. The fear that something may happen that we absolutely need to know about, just at the moment that we're navigating our way through a crowded street, keeps them clasped in our hands. We'll just take the odd glance at the screen from time to time, we tell ourselves, to ensure we haven't missed any notifications. Unfortunately, as we do this our attention immediately goes to the phone, not to our feet or our peripheral vision and – wham. It's not just the act of looking down at the screen that can cause us problems either; talking on a phone distracts our brains as much as messaging, some research suggests it might even be more. In one study of distracted walking injuries in the US, talking on the phone accounted for about 69 per cent of the injuries, compared to texting, which accounted for only about 9 per cent[3].

And then, there's the selfies.

Instagram's @influencersinthewild shows the ludicrous lengths influencers are prepared to go to for the perfect selfie or shot. But,

DISTRICT
ATTRACTED

Talking on the phone accounts for **69%** of walking injuries

being driven by the insatiable demands of the algorithm to take more and more extreme photos for their social media feed, is now literally causing people to die for 'likes'. A 2018 study of news reports uncovered 259 deaths caused by selfie taking between 2011 and 2017.

The trend for 'gender reveal' stunts for social media audiences (where an expectant couple reveal the gender of their unborn child) has also led to a steady rise in smartphone-related deaths. In 2019 a 56-year old grandmother in Des Moines was killed when a pipe bomb exploded as her family experimented with different types of explosives for a gender-reveal announcement they were filming to be posted on social media.

And a horrifying example of the perils of being totally engrossed by our smartphones is that the victims of the deadly Japanese volcano eruption at Mount Ontake in 2014 evidently spent their last minutes taking smartphone snaps instead of fleeing and saving themselves. Around half of the 56 bodies recovered were found clutching phones containing photos of the deadly ash and lava, taken in the final minutes of their lives.

We might be tempted to be dismissive of such extreme examples of the consequences of being distracted by our smartphones, of trying to get the perfect dramatic photo to pander to our followers. But each of us could easily take a wrong turn or a tumble while distracted by a phone. Apparently, more than half of all distracted walking incidents in the US happen in the home[4], not in, or by, a road. I wonder how many of you reading this know that you've already had an experience of this yourselves; of walking into a door, stumbling off a flight of stairs, hitting your head on a kitchen cupboard while being glued to your phone at home? Increasingly we live our lives utterly distracted by our screens, oblivious to what's happening right in front of us. In some cases that can put us in real physical danger, especially in places where we need to watch our step.

Let's be more aware of how much our phone distracts us when walking, even when that's in the supposedly safe environment of our own home. Avoid checking Google Maps every few seconds and try and plan a route in advance wherever possible. If we need to urgently take a call or reply to a message, move out of the way of other pedestrians and traffic, and stop before engaging in your smartphone. We've always taught children how to safely cross the street, by looking one way and then another before moving out into the road. That advice now needs to include putting their phones away when around traffic, or when needing to watch where they're going. We should all be heeding that advice, too.

Smombies [aka smartphone zombies]:
n. people who walk, glued to their smartphone, on autopilot, not looking where they are going and oblivious to their surroundings.

⚠ SIGNS:

Walking while talking (or texting or scrolling) on your smartphone, unaware of your surroundings. Regularly bumping into objects, falling over, causing minor (or major) accidents because you're not looking where you're going.

💡 SOLUTION:

Don't walk while texting or talking on your phone. It's as simple as that. In an attempt not to make this the shortest piece of advice from me in the book though, I'll add that in order to accomplish this you need to be smarter about where your phone is located as you walk. Don't have it in your hand. That makes it easy to steal as well as meaning you don't have two free hands to catch you should you fall. Don't have it in your jeans or coat pocket, where your wandering hands can alight upon it in seconds. Put it away in a zipped compartment in your bag or backpack. Put it right at the bottom of your bag, with lots of stuff heaped on top. Obviously, if you are using your phone to navigate, that's not very practical. In which case STOP every time you consult the route on your screen and stand utterly still. Set off again, putting your phone away, only when you know where you are going. Train yourself to think 'stop walking!' whenever you take your phone out on a pavement. Also, remember to be aware of your phone usage in your own home – you can just as easily walk into a door or cupboard while looking at your phone in your house as you can run into trouble out on a pavement.

ON CYBERCHONDRIA

'Doctors are so busy'

E mma was absolutely convinced that she had Lyme disease. She had been meticulously researching all her symptoms, medical forum by medical forum, for over a week now. Tiredness and loss of energy, tick. Muscle and joint pain, tick. Headache, tick. The only thing missing was a red rash, but there was that little rough patch of skin by her elbow, which might be a rash, if she examined it a bit more closely.

Then again, she had also been thinking that her symptoms might be a sign of rheumatoid arthritis. She had been feeling particularly stiff in the mornings, now she thought about it. Would that explain the lack of energy? Maybe... she had a very rare combination of both? The Lyme disease could be a more recent addition to the underlying slowly developing arthritis she might be suffering from?

Emma googled her symptoms late into the night, printing out page after page of descriptions and diagrams from the websites she consulted, which she put in a bulging plastic folder to discuss with her doctor.

Apparently the doctor was less than gracious, dismissing all of Emma's self diagnoses as baseless. It had been the fifth time in two months that Emma had convinced herself that some relatively innocuous symptom was evidence of a serious illness. Emma is by no means alone; 72 per cent of US internet users have searched for health information online in the past year, and 35 per cent of all US adults have tried to self-diagnose a medical condition using the internet with women much more likely than men to go online to figure out a possible diagnosis[1].

So, what do the doctors think?

'It's definitely happening more and more that patients are googling their health concerns and I think it's brilliant that they're doing it to be informed and take control of their health,' Dr Sophie Jukes, London GP, GP trainer and examiner for the Royal College of General Practitioners, told me. 'The problem is that Google is giving patients information about what the search engine thinks the patient wants, not necessarily what the patient needs; i.e. what the most likely diagnosis is.' This is then making the patient anxious and fixated on a dangerous untruth and no doubt falling deeper and deeper into a never-ending cycle of searching through online information.

Sophie gave me the example of a patient typing 'tingling symptoms' into Google. 'If you type that in, Google assumes you're worried about those symptoms and delivers you the most frequently read articles; those about Multiple Sclerosis (MS). In fact, the most common cause of tingling symptoms is usually a trapped nerve.' And most of those searching for health information are blindly taking the search results returned to them at face value, without questioning whether they are appropriate. Two-thirds of those looking for information on a health issue began their last inquiry on a search engine but only 15 per cent then checked the source and date of the information the search engine enquiry led them to[2].

'Google is really preying on the vulnerable with the way it works,' Sophie continued, 'it's more often the people who already have anxiety about all areas of their lives who do this sort of over-investigating of their health. It perpetuates their anxieties and makes their health concerns much worse. We have to unpick a lot of it when they turn up in the surgery to see us.' In fact, when asking US adults who searched for health information online, 10 per cent said they regularly feel anxiety and fear over medical information they find online[3].

We all like to think of ourselves as internet sleuths of one type or another. We believe we're all capable of uncovering just the right piece of information we need online, often at the expense of so-called 'experts' who might have missed an obscure point or condition. We can all find online people triumphantly exclaiming about something their doctor missed, which they diagnosed by googling information about their condition themselves.

Why shouldn't we be one of those people too, and diagnose ourselves with an obscure medical condition that our over-worked

Dr G🔍gle Will See You Now

doctors have missed? There are two reasons why this miraculous insight is unlikely to be blessed upon most of us.

The first is that one of the things that happens when we go online to search for anything, is that in carrying out a piece of research, we invariably fall prey to a condition called 'confirmation bias', which is the tendency to look for information, opinions and points of view that support something we already believe.

So, you're feeling a little anxious about your health and starting to suspect that there must be something terribly wrong with you, you go online to investigate and bingo, on Page One of Google you find links to what you suspected all along, that you are at death's door. This is made all the more likely if you google 'bad headaches, brain tumour' or 'bad headaches, dying'.

The second problem is the reliability of the medical and health information you find online. Anyone with any qualifications (often,

Over 25% of British women have misdiagnosed ♡ themselves

that means none) can set up a health or wellness website and publish information, which is at best unreliable, at worst dangerous. Enthusiastic reviews can be faked, miraculous cures can be conjured up, qualifications and certifications can be invented. Of the American health sites analysed by NewsGuard, which rates the reliability of news and information websites, 11 per cent publish false or unfounded health claims[4]. And because most people don't understand that search engine results can be manipulated, very often the top search results for your enquiry, which you might think ought to be the most reputable, can take you to a site that contains health information that is absolute rubbish.

At the pretty harmless end of the scale, websites like these can tell you that a particular diet or food group is the answer to your health concerns. At the more worrying end, you can be convinced you have a life-limiting condition, and you may be preyed upon to spend thousands of pounds on scams or fake cures, once you believe this. According to one 2012 study[5], over one-quarter of British women have misdiagnosed themselves on the internet, then bought the wrong product or drug to try and cure their illness. A fifth have at one time wrongly suspected they have a serious disease, with breast cancer and other forms of cancer topping the list of the most common false alarms after a misdiagnosis online.

Being able to consult 'Dr Google' at the touch of a button can have its benefits and prompt you to see a health professional, but the internet should never be your primary resource. Instead of well-meaning attempts to put less pressure on the health service, cyberchondria is unfortunately actually doing the opposite. The impact on the British healthcare system is estimated to be costing £56 million a year through booking further GP appointments and tests to try and prove the diagnoses offered by Dr Google[6]. Additionally, if people are misdiagnosing conditions and are self-treating, they could be causing themselves and others long-term harm.

There's a wealth of really valuable, useful and reputable health information online so by all means keep yourself informed, but always check who the website is owned and operated by and particularly the qualifications and credentials of anyone giving advice. This area of the internet is one where you really can't be too careful about who you are taking advice from. Our health anxieties are often preyed upon, with some popular 'health' websites having strong links to pharmaceutical and other companies, meaning that your fears are played with and you're directed to purchasing pills that you may not need at all. These websites and Big Pharma are profiting off of your fears; it's time to put a stop to this once and for all. Avoid the lure of Dr Google and instead book an appointment with a trusted, impartial healthcare professional. Your physical and mental health will be the better for it.

Cyberchondria [aka consulting Dr Google]:

n. the unfounded escalation of concerns about common and/or minor physical symptoms based on search results and material found online.

⚠ SIGNS:

Obsessive googling of minor physical symptoms, becoming convinced they are a sign of a major health issue with significantly raised anxiety levels as a result. Doing this repeatedly for a range of different symptoms over a sustained period of time – i.e. not just the normal tendency to seek out health-related information online.

☼ SOLUTION:

If you already suffer from anxiety, investigating health symptoms online is not a good idea. Limit yourself in both frequency and duration of searches. If you feel anxiety levels rising, stop. Don't 'lead' the research results by adding words like 'fatal', 'cancer', 'death' to your enquiries. Keep your searches neutral. Understand that the top-listed results for any health-related search engine enquiries may not feature the most reliable medical sources. A much better approach: don't begin your health enquiry with an internet search, go directly to reputable websites and look within their published content. If you do find yourself looking at other websites or forums, cross-check the qualifications of the medical professionals and how relevant those qualifications are to the subject they are discussing. Understand that many posters in health forums may have an agenda that may be to sell you something or increase your fear about your health (see also 'Fake News', page 30). Make a consultation with your primary care physician as soon as you can to discuss any symptoms that are worrying you.

ON TECH-LIFE
BALANCE

'I get all my best ideas
after midnight'

was struggling with a new client: a huge global partnership, headquartered in a vertiginous glass tower, had hired me for a month-long digital wellbeing project.

Yet, I had the strong suspicion that most of the older partners were just paying lip service to the idea of work-life balance. They had no intention of seriously changing how they worked, and the junior members of their firm knew it. As a result, it all felt a bit lacklustre, like one big pointless box-ticking exercise. But Ben was different. In his late 30s, newly made partner and responsible for one of the regional offices, his enthusiasm was palpable.

He was full of ideas on how he, and his mostly young-ish team of lawyers, could get a better balance with tech. A technophile himself, he'd invested in all the latest software to help them all keep on top of their workload. I had groaned slightly to myself when he mentioned Slack; a project management software tool which, once installed, grows like an invasive garden weed and is just as knotty to remove. In my experience, everyone begins to really resent it as it takes over every aspect of their lives, but no one ever quite knows how to disentangle themselves.

Ben invited me to a round-table discussion in Bristol where I would chair a team talk about what they could all do to improve their work-life balance. The concept of work-life balance was one that was completely thrown on its head when the birth of the smartphone, umbilical cord to our workplace, disrupted our lives. The lure of flexible working reeled us in with the idea we could work at any time, in any place. But the result is we now work all the time, from every place.

Reading and replying to emails just during the working day now seems an anachronism when hardly anyone respects what used to be called 'office hours'. More than three-quarters (81 per cent) of US adults[1] say they check their work email on weekends; 55 per cent check emails after 11pm; 59 per cent check emails on vacation; and 58 per cent admit they regularly check their work email in bed just after waking up[2]. A worrying 6 per cent admit to even having checked their emails at a funeral. The result is that nearly half of all working adults in one study said they considered themselves workaholics[3], perhaps because they were confusing an inability to switch off from their smartphone with true workaholism, which is defined by an innate, inner drive to keep working.

Sadly, we have no comparative statistics from before the smartphone era ('workaholism' was only coined as a word in 1971), but my guess would be that far fewer people identified themselves this way before the era of computing. The coronavirus pandemic further piled on workplace pressures: in one 2020 study of US and European adults working remotely, 60 per cent said they felt they were expected to always be online and contactable to prove they're working to their manager[4].

In Bristol, we kicked off with a few easy wins. Cc'ing and bcc'ing of emails had got out of control everyone agreed. No one wanted to be included in endless email chains, which had only a passing relevance to them. The endless niceties of 'thank you' and 'no, you're welcome' emails that are particularly endemic in UK 'techiquette' were doing no favours in clogging up inboxes and could reasonably be eliminated, without the firm descending into complete anarchy.

Things were progressing smoothly. But some of the younger members of the team had been noticeably quiet. Emily, a woman in her early 20s, had been clearly trying to judge the right moment to speak. I paused to look over at her and she launched in.

'I wondered if we could talk about your weekend emails, Ben?'

There was a slight ripple around the large boardroom-style table, and I noticed a few relieved and grateful looks being shot at the young woman speaking.

'The ones you send late at night on a Saturday. They always leave me stressed when they appear. I spend most of the night and all of Sunday worrying about what I need to get done on Monday when I get back into work.'

Ben looked a bit puzzled. 'But I always mark them "no need for a response". I'm pretty sure I usually put "Do not read until Monday" too?' He looked at the rest of them for their confirmation.

81% of US adults

say they check their work email on weekends

Emily was squirming in her seat and looking like she really wished she had gone with her first instinct and kept her mouth shut.

'I think I can see what the problem might be,' I interjected. 'When you put "no need to read" or "don't respond" Ben, the team are still reading them, because they feel they should. Or, because they just can't bring themselves to ignore them. It is hard for junior members of any team to ignore an email from someone senior to them, whatever that person might say, when they're trying to impress them, and keep their job.' Ben looked genuinely amazed.

'But I get all my best ideas after midnight. I just bang them out in an email, so I don't forget them. Then everyone can get going with them on Monday without wasting any time.'

The discussion that followed was as animated as it was needed. It was clear that Ben was respected by his close-knit team and that they genuinely liked him. It was equally clear he was a committed people manager who wanted to help them all get on in their careers and deliver really good service to their clients.

By firing off his nocturnal emails, he thought he was arming them with the tools they needed to succeed. He hadn't realized he was actually adding to their stress and preventing them from getting much-needed downtime.

The solution was simple when we arrived at it. Ben would still keep writing the nocturnal missives, but he would leave them in his email drafts folder and only hit 'send' at 8am Monday morning. That way he could still record his flashes of inspiration and the team could come back to work recharged and ready to work on them.

The French get a lot of things right. Since 2017 they've had enshrined in law a 'Right to Disconnect', which gives employees the legal right to ignore emails after working hours. As a result of everyone working from home in the pandemic, struggling to keep family and work lives separate, there have been more calls globally to follow the example of the French. In April 2021, a policy was enshrined into the employment Code of Practice in Ireland, granting all workers the right to disconnect electronically at the end of the working day. There are also proposals currently being discussed to include it in the new UK Employment Bill. Perhaps the experience of working during a pandemic has finally presented workplaces with the conversation-opener they needed to address this issue.

If you're not in a country which is taking the issue of work-life balance seriously, you will need to be a bit more proactive. Often software itself has a feature that can solve some of the problems we might have in using it. What we must all accept is that none of these tools are a replacement for effective communication and connection. It's up to all of us to write the rules for how we use technology in a way that enhances, not diminishes, our lives to avoid burnout and an imbalance in our work and home life.

Tech-Life Balance:

n. using technology in a way that doesn't have a negative effect on your personal life or relationships.

⚠ SIGNS:

You can't remember when you last had a holiday without being umbilically connected to the office via email. You routinely send and receive emails at the weekend and after 11pm at night in the week. You check your email before you check your partner in the morning.

💡 SOLUTION:

Start a conversation in your workplace about out-of-hours emails. The chances are everyone feels the same way but doesn't want to be the one to bring it up. Every workplace I've worked in has agreed that the tyranny of 24:7 emails needs to stop. One thing you can do right now is to commit to sending less emails yourself. The more you send the more you receive. (One estimate says we receive 1.75 to 2 emails for every one we send.)

Switch to voice calls for the simple stuff. Stop cc-ing and bcc-ing everyone. Opt out of unnecessary email chains and groups. Batch-checking emails has been proven to improve efficiency and productivity. Set two or three fixed times a day when you will check emails, then log off. Communicate this clearly to your colleagues and give them a number to ring you, if it's a genuine emergency. Everyone thinks twice before phoning but emailing at the weekend somehow feels less invasive, which is why we all do it.

If you have staff reporting to you, think hard about your own habits. A decade ago, if your boss had shown up on your doorstep at the weekend to chat about what needed to be done in the office, you would have been horrified. When we email someone less senior at the weekend, that's exactly what we're doing. We're inviting ourselves into their personal space and interrupting their rest. Don't do it.

ON DOOMSCROLLING

'Like falling down
a rabbit hole'

'I scroll through tweets and news articles constantly, then I can't get to sleep worrying about the pandemic, the job losses, the protests.'

'I'm trying to focus on work, but then I keep picking up my phone to check how many more people have died.'

'My parents constantly post links to infection statistics and hospital capacity scares in case the rest of us have missed them. My heart rate raises now every time I see a new notification.'

'I set up a Sky News alert on my phone right at the beginning of the pandemic and now I wish I hadn't – I can't drag myself away from it.'

Paula read out a stream of anxious messages to me from her marketing department's group chat. She had booked a webinar with me to help her team during lockdown. It was January 2021, and the world was still at the mercy of the coronavirus pandemic with new, ever-more contagious strains being discovered. 'They want to know if you can cover anything on being unable to stop checking the news?' Paula asked.

I was happy to oblige. The first step was to offer that there is absolutely nothing wrong with wanting to stay informed. However doomscrolling, or doomsurfing, is different: it is an endless doom-and-gloom spiral of scrolling, clicking, refreshing and jumping from one shocking story to the next harrowing headline. It consumes you until you're so deep into that bottomless black hole it feels like you cannot climb out of it.

During the coronavirus pandemic the number of us obsessively checking the news – specifically bad news – escalated to new levels. A worldwide pandemic, brutally policed George Floyd protests and the divisive 2020 US Election all came together in a perfect storm to exacerbate this bad habit. We don't have any research yet on how many of us were affected, but #doomscrolling was a trending hashtag on Twitter for weeks at a time in 2020 after Karen Ho, a finance reporter from Quartz, took it upon herself to issue a gentle daily nudge to stop other Twitter users from doing it.

Like many of us, Paula's team was seeking answers, reassurance and clarity through relentless research. Unaided by cunning algorithms feeding their seemingly masochistic interests, they didn't find this. What they did discover is that an unremitting torrent of bad news is bad news for mental health. Their compulsive news-reading habits made them feel anxious, hopeless, sleepless and low.

Bad news has always made us feel bad. While most US adults (95 per cent) say they follow the news regularly, 56 per cent say that doing so causes them stress[1]. Similarly, a UK study in 2011 found viewing negative news on TV increased sad and anxious moods in viewers[2]. But, for reasons we don't yet completely understand, research from the earliest days of the coronavirus pandemic in China[3] seems to show that the consumption of stressful content online appears to have a worse effect than consuming it elsewhere. In the research, viewing bad news online was specifically associated with negative psychological outcomes and depression, to a degree not seen in 'traditional' media use.

Paula's team was exhausted and entirely aware of the erosion to their wellbeing, so why couldn't they stop?

In the pre-digital world, traditional print editors knew that outrageous, attention-grabbing headlines sold newspapers. Entire careers were made by honing this skill, which materializes online as 'clickbait' – teaser lines that will bait a user to click through to a specific website to read the full story. And it's not uplifting news that grabs our attention unfortunately. An old newspaper adage used to be that a thousand planes landing safely isn't a news story, but the one plane that doesn't, is. It's bad news, not good, which has always sold newspapers, prompted viewers to turn on the TV and now makes us click on a link. One theory is that in our hunter gatherer days we had to be more attuned to threats in our environment than joys; otherwise, caught up in the pleasure of the sunrise we might not notice the charging bison.

Our masochistic instincts are to pay more attention to bad news online than good. We click on negative links with much greater

ENDLESS DOOM-AND-GLOOM SCROLLING ENDLESS DOOM-AND-GLOOM SCROLLING ENDLESS DOOM-AND-GLOOM SCROLLING ENDLESS DOOM-AND-GLOOM SCROLLING ENDLESS DOOM-AND-GLOOM SCROLLING ENDLESS DOOM-AND-GLOOM SCROLLING

frequency than positive ones as lab experiments have shown[4]. In one experiment, even when people expressly said they preferred to read good news, they exhibited a bias towards choosing news stories with a negative tone, rather than neutral or positive stories. People who were more interested in current affairs and politics were particularly likely to choose the bad news. Hungry online algorithms then observe our online behaviour and amplify the impact of our negative news bias by serving up more of what they think we're looking for. Google's *RankBrain*, the system which determines its search rankings, is driven by machine learning, or AI, which evaluates the 'user intent' behind each user search, regardless of the specific words used. Google's RankBrain says in effect, 'hmm, you've

While 95% of US adults say 📰 they follow the news regularly, 56% ⚡ say it causes them stress

searched just for "news", but what is it you're *really* looking for?' Because the number of other people who have previously visited a page is part of how Google decides its relevance, a search on 'news' will always return the currently most popular stories ranked the most highly. And, because of our preference for the negative, these are almost always, drum roll, bad news stories.

It's hardly surprising that consuming a non-stop stream of bad news makes us feel bad. But the bigger problem is that it may actually give us a very distorted picture of the state of the world.

If we read bad news story after bad news story, we may begin to believe that the world is all bad, that nothing good is happening or will ever happen again, and that the planet is on a downward spiral of doom. All the carefully completed gratitude journals in the world can't pull us out of a tailspin of depressing thoughts, if we're constantly chasing tales of an ever-nearing apocalypse across the internet.

A global pandemic, our bad-news-seeking propensity, and a clickbait digital news environment make for a heady toxic combination, and the perfect storm to breed doomscrolling. Paula's team was as susceptible as any of us. I assured them that while doomscrolling was a difficult online pitfall, it wasn't one they needed to fall in to. Paying attention to their mood both before and after news-checking and setting strict limits on how and when they checked news was going to be key. Common sense was required, for example realizing that ending your day with the news would make it hard to switch off at a time you should be winding down.

They would also have to give up deluding themselves that they were doing it to be well informed. Unless you work in the news industry yourself there is absolutely no need to be checking news 24:7. Dip in, get your update, then log off and go and do something productive. News websites are going to up the ante to try and get you to visit more frequently, and headlines will get more and more lurid to entice you to click. The news does not stop. In fact, it never sleeps. But you can, and you need to.

Doomscrolling will not prevent the bad events and statistics from happening. It cannot offer the information tonic you desire. It won't calm you down when you're looking for reassurance. In the 1970s, the 'Mean World Syndrome'[5] discovered that heavy and repeated viewing of stories of violence on TV left people perceiving the world to be a more dangerous place than it actually was. The more you consume bad news, the more worried and anxious you become about the world around you. Doomscrolling will leave you overwhelmed, uncomfortable and catastrophizing. Consume slowly, sparingly and sufficiently.

Doomscrolling [aka doomsurfing]:
v. consuming an endless amount of negative news stories online.

⚠ SIGNS:

Finding yourself compulsively drawn to checking bad news online. Scrolling deeper and deeper into upsetting, depressing and negative news, unable to switch off as your mood deteriorates.

⚙️ SOLUTION:

Switch off breaking news story alerts on your devices; you'll get a more balanced story a few hours after any story breaks, when more facts are gathered, and the evidence has been assessed. If you remove the easy access to news sites, you will eliminate the possibility of it popping up on your phone as an alert and it will take some of the urgency out of having to be up-to-date. Set limits for yourself for news checking. Don't check news late at night when you are tired, and emotions are running high. The old adage that everything looks better in the morning applies to the news, too.

Make a point of searching out good news online and resetting your personal content algorithm. There are plenty of websites that make it their business to tell us all the good stuff that's happening in the world. When the urge to check the news hits, look at one of those instead. As you click more and more on good news and uplifting stories, you'll be served up more and more of these. If enough of us do it, we could re-design how news works online. But let's not hold our breath.

ON CLICKTIVISM

———

'Hashtags are so lazy'

Nicky was standing in Trafalgar Square, at the end of the day-long march through London's streets, when she noticed Katy had posted a picture of the distinctive banner right in front of her on social media. She wheeled round scanning the crowd, but couldn't see her friend anywhere.

'Where are you??' she texted. 'I'm right by that banner!' There was no reply from Katy, but a few minutes later she noticed the picture had been deleted.

'When I met up with her about a week later, it turned out she wasn't even there!' she exclaimed. 'And yet, all her socials that day were full of posts about the march. She'd even changed her profile pic that morning to the one with the march logo. It's not that she ever actually said she was there, but her feed gave the strong impression she was.

'I shouldn't have been surprised. She's always jumping on the latest hashtag, and hashtags are so lazy.'

Nicky went on to tell me about all the different hashtags Katy had enthusiastically shared over the last few years – #MeToo, #TimesUp, #BLM were just a few.

'The #ChallengeAccepted campaign irritated me the most though. Women simply posted hot black and white photos of themselves. When Katy posted one, I hadn't a clue what it was all about. When I looked into it, I found it was originally started in Turkey to raise awareness of femicide. By the time Katy was sharing it though, I don't think she had any idea about that. I think she just thought it was some generic female empowerment effort.'

I'm uncomfortably aware that I've done this, too. I've changed my profile pic many times over the years to one with a filter or badge, highlighting my support for a particular cause. And I've used more than a few hashtags in my time. As Nicky was talking, I cringed at this, making a mental note to clamp down on that kind of performative posting.

Why do we do it? Why do we get caught up in trending hashtags and share and post about causes and campaigns, then quickly move onto something else without following through with any real action or commitment?

Part of the reason is the ridiculously low bar to entry. It's just so easy. Adding a 'like' to a post or retweeting and sharing a logo or sentiment takes next to no effort compared to putting our hands in our pockets to make a donation, or turning up in person to volunteer for a cause.

And we get quite a lot of payback in doing it. Displaying visual badges of causes we support online is a bit like showing what we're all about in how we dress, the car we drive, or how we furnish our homes. Online acts of support for good causes signal our virtuousness and selflessness to others. Our digital virtue signalling is us waving a little flag online that says, 'Look at me, over here, look! See what a good person I am.'

This kind of support is shallow. Evidence shows that the ease and superficiality of so much of the digital world is turning us into people who are eager to show how we champion good causes online but often without very much knowledge or understanding of what they are really all about.

In the Stork Fountain experiment in 2009, Danish lecturer Anders Colding-Jørgensen set out to see how many people he could get to engage on social media with a fictitious cause. He set up a Facebook group 'No to Demolition of Stork Fountain', claiming the famous Stork Fountain in Copenhagen, Denmark, was about to be razed to the ground to make way for a clothing store. Even though he clearly explained in the discussion forum on the page that it was a social experiment and that the fountain wasn't in any real danger, most people didn't read it, they just went ahead and joined the group anyway. This was the very early days of social media, yet he still managed to get 27,000 Danish supporters for his fake petition after just two weeks.

Of course, clicktivism can have its advantages; in sharing a hashtag, image or call to action, you can amplify little-known ideas and communicate non-mainstream concepts. Clicktivism can be

#ISTHIS ENOUGH?

argued to have helped to further the aims and visibility of Occupy Wall Street, Black Lives Matter and #MeToo, to name just a few. But, retweeting and re-posting can only take us so far. One estimate puts the percentage of the membership of any online group who will ever take action on the cause they have joined, at a pitiful 1–5 per cent[1]. A particularly squirm-inducing example was an incredibly popular Facebook group, 'Saving the children of Africa', which was revealed in 2009 to have over 1.2 million members who in total had donated only $6,000 to the cause (i.e. half a cent per person)[2].

Only 1–5%
will take action on the cause they have joined

An important question is what happens to us once we've shown our support for a cause by joining such a campaigning group, signing an online petition or changing our profile pic? Maybe our social virtue signalling is just the first step, but doesn't it then inspire us to do something more for the cause?

One issue seems to be that once we've joined a bigger group, we succumb to something that's been called 'social loafing', where individuals exert themselves less when in a group compared to when they're working alone. The same thing happens when we share those hashtags, change those profile pics or when disingenuous brands post little black squares. When we become part of a group, all ostensibly working together towards the same cause, it appears we feel we don't actually have to do very much about it ourselves. There must be lots of people all doing the real work, we reason; we're just here showing that we're right behind them, cheering them on in their efforts. We need to make sure that we're properly investing ourselves in the causes we're interested in, and not leave it to others.

Back with Nicky, I couldn't help but sympathize with her irritation at Katy's endless posting on social media without any real-world action. I suggested that Nicky could engage with Katy more, see what issues Katy really cares about. That way, she could help Katy turn her obvious enthusiasm for social causes into something more involved. Nicky could try and work out what Katy feels passionate about, and encourage her to take more action there, without pressurising her. Some people may not feel comfortable or have the confidence and time to volunteer in person. Instead of making activism competitive (some people think that even marches and protests don't effect much change), we can encourage, rather than discourage, others to help out in whatever way they can. But, while we do that, let's all try to motivate each other to step up and make meaningful change happen, instead of jumping on a hashtag by default.

When any of us think about the online payback we get for visibly supporting a cause, compared to the real-world payback we might get if we got really involved, it might make us all pause for thought. Actively giving back improves our wellbeing like few other activities; just one act of kindness, once a week over a six-week period, noticeably improves the mental wellbeing of the giver[3]. We're not going to get the same boost from just clicking a like button or adding a trending hashtag to a tweet. Discuss issues you're interested in with friends and family, publicize the causes you're passionate about and see how you can get involved outside of the social media realm. Use your online engagement as a platform to real world action and see the power of your passion and commitment. It may be far more effort to get involved with physical volunteering but the reward, both for the recipients and ourselves, is far greater.

Clicktivism [aka slacktivism]:

n. the practice of supporting a political or social cause via the internet by means such as social media or online petitions, typically characterized as involving minimal effort or commitment.

⚠ SIGNS:

You're a clicktivist when you use hashtags, change your profile pic, share or retweet sentiments, all of which promote a political or social cause, but don't follow this up with any meaningful effort to effect change in the real world.

💡 SOLUTION:

If you want people to engage in your cause, make it hard for them to display their badges or trophies of identity until they have made a meaningful contribution. Design specific, non-trivial, tasks that can be farmed out to willing supporters and measured; that way there can be no hiding behind a generalized hashtag or banner. To avoid social loafing, always link named individuals with specific goals.

If you think you might be guilty of clicktivism yourself, make a conscious effort to stop jumping on online bandwagons and making meaningless digital gestures. It has to be an active choice and awareness on your part. Think carefully about the causes you want to support and work out how to actively help them reach their goals. It's quite hard to resist the social pressure to share badges and hashtags so you could start by explaining to everyone that this is what you've decided to do. Being vocal about your intentions and actions will help keep you accountable. And you can check any strategy you adopt by asking those who are most directly impacted by the movement you support, what action is most useful to them. I can guarantee it won't be retweeting hashtags.

ON NOMOPHOBIA

———

'What if someone
needs me?'

I wasn't surprised to get the phone call. I could rely on getting at least one a couple of days before each digital detox weekend. I host these retreats annually and panicked calls have become part of the process. But this time I was surprised by who the call came from.

Guilia was the European head of a US-owned media company. In her mid-30s and with a young child, she had a demanding workload and had been signed off work for burnout in the role before her current one. She had been enthusiastic when she had booked to join us for a long weekend in a beautiful *masseria* (farmhouse) in Puglia, southern Italy, at the end of the month. 'It's exactly what I need, a proper break, I can't wait!' she had signed-off in her confirmation email.

'Listen, I know it's not strictly allowed,' she murmured conspiratorially down the phone to me now, 'but I'll need to have my phone in my bedroom to check in between our activities. I promise I won't let anyone else know, I won't get it out in any of the public areas of the *masseria*.'

I took a small breath, trying to sound as soothing as possible. 'Of course, I absolutely understand your worries, Guilia, lots of people feel panic just before the weekend. But giving up your smartphone is the whole point of the retreat. If I let you keep it, I'd have to let everyone else do it. And if you did keep it, you wouldn't get any of the benefits of coming. You'd just be wasting your money...'

I went through my fairly practised routine to assuage her concerns, pointing out that she would in fact still be contactable. 'You may not have noticed on the email I sent you, but there's a landline at the farmhouse that you can give to anyone who needs to get hold of you. So, you see, everyone can ring you as normal, just on the landline not on your phone.'

She paused, possibly ruminating on the startling idea that landlines still existed.

'But what if we're not actually at the farmhouse? There are walks planned, what if I'm doing one of those and someone needs me, and they can't get hold of me?' Her breathing was getting noticeably quicker.

'Well, yes, we are away from the house a bit over the weekend, but I think the longest we'd be completely away would only be for about an hour and a half.'

She took that all in, then tried another tack. 'It's actually not just about calls, I may be sent something via email that I need to read and respond to.'

I could definitely hear in her voice that she was now feeling more than a little panicked as she faced the reality of being completely without her phone.

'Well, we arrive Thursday night, so Friday is actually the only full working day you'd be without email. Do you have a secretary? Do they have access to your email?'

Guilia confirmed that she had not one, but two, secretaries and that both of them had access to her email account.

'That's great!' I exclaimed, thinking at this stage that we had cracked it. 'They can check your email for you. If there's anything you absolutely need to respond to, they can ring the landline at the house and go through your reply.'

I really didn't want to encourage Guilia to be tethered to her work for the weekend, but I was hoping that by talking through how an emergency situation could work she would feel more relaxed about the prospect of being without her phone.

This fear of being without your smartphone has a neat little name all of its own, *nomophobia*, and it has been around for as long as smartphones have. It was first coined as a term by British researchers in 2008 (yes, that's a mere year after the launch of the iPhone). One study[1] found that the percentage of people who feared being without their phone was as high as 66 per cent. Interestingly, the same study found more women worry about being without their phones than men – 70 per cent of the women surveyed compared to 61 per cent of the men – and that those aged 18–24 were the most nomophobic group, followed by those aged

I just CAN'T BE without my PHONE

25–34. The study also shows that in four years, between 2008 and 2012, in the US the proportion of the population who identified as suffering from nomophobia grew by 11 per cent.

I risked voicing what was going through my head as we had been talking. 'Look, Guilia, I hope you don't mind me saying this, but from everything you've told me, I think you would really benefit from this retreat. It sounds like you need to take just a couple of days to focus on yourself and not worry about anyone else; to completely switch off.'

This wasn't my first chat with Guilia. I had met her before at a public workshop I'd given. She explained that she was now alcohol-free, doing yoga three times a week and not eating dairy or gluten but was still suffering overwhelming periods of stress. 'So, the only thing you haven't tried is putting down your phone?' I prompted gently. As we had been talking, two smartphones ('One for work,

66% of us fear being without our phone

one for home') lay on the table in front of her. She had been touching them both reflexively as we chatted.

Guilia interrupted my thoughts, 'Look, I'm really sorry but I think I'm going to have to cancel.' She was now sounding relieved, as it had dawned on her she didn't have to go through with it. 'As I said, if it had been any other weekend it would have been totally fine, but I just can't be without my phone this time.'

I really regretted that Guilia wasn't with us that weekend. Without the constant interruptions from their smartphones and the pings of notifications, everyone agreed they felt calmer, more focused and completely relaxed. More than one person said at the end they felt they had been away for a whole week, not just for a weekend. They all agreed that although they had all been quite anxious beforehand at the prospect of being without their phones, the experience had been nowhere near as stressful as they had imagined. In fact, it hadn't been stressful at all.

I kept in touch with Guilia for a couple of years after that. There were a few more occasions when she enquired about coming with us, but she never again came as close as booking a weekend. I discovered much later that she had had to leave her current job after suffering from a very bad bout of burnout, taking six months completely out of the working world. Mutual friends told me that she was overhauling all aspects of her lifestyle and looking again at how she dealt with stress. I really hoped that she would make a connection between burnout and her phone habits.

Nomophobia is a condition that doesn't just impact our relationship with our phones, it spreads its tentacles into all areas of our lives. Research from Spain suggests that nomophobia negatively affects personality, self-esteem, anxiety, stress and academic performance[2].

Our daily lives have become much more stressful since the advent of the always-on digital world. Smartphones offer us constant connection to our family, our friends, to breaking news stories, to the world's finest entertainment sources, to the rewards of our work. They're designed to be stimulating, to keep us coming back for more. But while bursts of stimulation may be invigorating, non-stop stimulation drains us. The world may be digital but our brains are not, they need periods of downtime to recharge. If we fail to prioritize downtime, our brains start to falter. They begin to work less efficiently. We find ourselves struggling with focus and concentration, our short-term memory wavers and our decision-making deteriorates. Over-stimulation leads to stress and prolonged stress leads to burnout.

We all need to wrestle with our own budding nomophobia that has us believing that if we risk a trip outside our front door without our smartphone something terrible will happen. The same fear that has us scrolling in the bath and on the toilet, keeping our smartphones tightly clutched to us at all times, touching them reflexively in our pockets to make sure they're still there. If we don't learn how to separate ourselves from the tiny tyrant and its constant stimulation, we risk increased episodes of anxiety, stress, burnout, or worse.

Nomophobia:

n. an excessive and unreasonable fear of being without a mobile phone, of being beyond phone contact.

⚠ SIGNS:

Often associated with separation anxiety, nomophobia comes with a set of identifiable symptoms: increased heart rate and blood pressure, shortness of breath, anxiety, nausea, trembling, dizziness, depression, discomfort, fear and panic. You may find yourself excessively touching your phone; patting your pocket and bag over and again to check your phone is still there, even when you've just checked it; or panicking badly when you don't know where your phone is. There is debate among the medical community on its classification; nomophobia is described variously as a phobia, anxiety disorder, lifestyle disorder or even an addiction.

☀ SOLUTION:

The only way to deal with the fear of being without your phone is to de-sensitize yourself to it in small stages. Planning for an entire weekend off without your phone is likely to feel overwhelming if you haven't even tried it for an hour. I first experimented with a short, essential trip: going to the corner shop to buy milk and leaving my phone behind. I then built up to longer and longer phone-free excursions. The panic you feel anticipating this has no relationship to how uncomfortable you will actually find it. However, the only way you're going to know that is to try it, so I'm afraid it's a bit chicken and egg. As with so many things, trying it out is much easier if you don't go it alone. Find a friend and do it together. Perhaps make a plan to ditch your phones at similar times over a weekend so you can then catch up and compare notes on how it went. I should warn you though, people do get quite evangelical about how good they feel without their phone, so prepare to become one of 'those' people.

ON FILTER BUBBLES

'Who ARE all
these people?'

The seminar room was buzzing when I walked in the door that morning, the excitable chatter quite unlike anything that had greeted me before. But I was pretty sure the level of animation had nothing to do with the workshop on digital habits I was about to deliver.

It was Friday 24th June in London, and the outcome of the referendum on the UK's membership of the European Union had just been announced. This room of City workers were reeling at the Leave result and appeared more than a little confused by it.

'I don't know a single person who voted Leave,' exclaimed one woman. 'Everybody I know voted Remain,' nodded another in agreement. 'My Facebook feed is full this morning of people asking if anyone knows just *one* person who voted Leave,' added someone sitting at the back of the room. 'Who *are* all these people?'

It was clear that the huge disparity between what the seminar attendees had been seeing online in the lead up to the vote and the outcome of the referendum, was dominating all their thoughts that morning. I decided on the spur of the moment to scrap what I was planning to say in favour of a discussion about the phenomenon of filter bubbles online so that we could all open up a conversation about what might have happened.

The term filter bubble was coined by Eli Pariser in his book of the same name in 2012, to describe what happens when we find ourselves cocooned in a cosy bubble of people who share our world view, effectively 'filtering' out any opposing opinions. He gave a TED talk about it in May 2011 and ever since the term has been enthusiastically co-opted to explain increasing social and political polarization, both online and off.

So, what's the truth behind filter bubbles?

Well, they almost certainly do exist offline. Our filter bubbles are built up over time and are dictated by our upbringing, education, financial circumstances and occupation. Most of us probably find ourselves living in an area with people who look and sound just like us, who have been educated in the same way, attended the same schools, do the same jobs, all of which can make us oblivious to the lives and views of people who may live only a few miles away. Research by Facebook found that for every four out of five Facebook friends you have with the same views as you, you only have one with opposing views[1]. But isn't this true of life as a whole? That we generally cluster with people who think like us?

Those who argue for the existence of digital filter bubbles say they are forming with more intensity and impact online because of the way we now get our news and how search and social media algorithms work. They can definitely have their advantages because they're a way of connecting with individuals who have the same interests and passions as us. The disadvantages become clear when we're looking to stimulate our creativity and consider alternative viewpoints. In filter bubbles, there is no room for things that provoke discomfort or point us towards ideas different to our own. How are we expected to be able to have healthy debates when our opinions become so entrenched?

If they do exist, we don't really have hard evidence yet for how much they are impacting on our view of the world. The Reuters Institute for the Study of Journalism at Oxford University say they have found five different studies worldwide since 2014 that show either 'no, or weak, evidence' for the existence of filter bubbles, two that show 'mixed evidence' and none so far for very strong evidence.

The Reuters Institute have been collecting data on how we all get our news since 2012. Their Digital News Report is the world's largest annual survey of news audiences and surveys 80,000 people across 40 different countries to get a clear picture of global news-gathering trends. They've found that if you're over 45 you're still most likely to get your news from TV, but if you're under 45 it's now social media. Facebook is still the domain platform globally for social media news gathering, but both Instagram and WhatsApp have seen big growth in recent years. Instagram is now predicted to outpace Twitter for news gathering before too long and WhatsApp has grown from 10 per cent using it for news to 16 per cent since they started the survey.

When I talk about using WhatsApp for news I don't just mean the growth of news organizations, such as *The New York Times* and *The Telegraph*, using WhatsApp groups for sharing their news stories; what I'm also talking about is the habit we all have of sending each other links, images and videos within messages and posting them to groups we're in (also see 'Fake News', page 30). We also see and share news when we send links or videos within Facebook Messenger, and we see links friends and family have posted on their Facebook pages or in their Instagram stories. Clicking on any of these links, or viewing gifs or videos, leads us to the news content that informs our view of the world.

Because of the way social media algorithms work, content that gets prioritized on our feeds tends to be very similar to things we've already engaged with before. If we've liked, shared or commented on something from *The New York Times* via Facebook (maybe commenting on a post a friend has shared), we'll see stories from *The New York Times* again, next time we're on Facebook. Similarly, if we've liked something from Fox News, we'll get more posts from that channel. However, Reuters Institute found that people do this for themselves offline as well. One of their first studies found that when people are getting their news offline, they stick to just one or two news sources they prefer, and don't deviate from them much at all.

So, it appears our social media feed is just giving us the news we want, and what we'd choose for ourselves offline anyway. But in doing that, is it leaving out a really important part of being human, which is the experience of discovery; coming across content, an opinion or a news story, you could never in a million years have predicted you would like, but which somehow touches a nerve and chimes with you, even altering your world view as a result? Before we romanticize that idea too much, it's worth bearing in mind that we may never have been all that good at doing this for ourselves, given the number of articles, books and programmes devoted to the subject of getting us all out of our comfort zones.

Are there any other areas of online news gathering that might be herding us into filter bubbles against our will? Well, one study looking at what happens when we search on Google, or another search engine, by political party in the US, found that search results for Democrats and Republicans were more or less identical[2]. So, the idea that if you're a Democrat and you only get left-leaning results when you're searching for news was debunked by that one piece of research. However, the SplitScreen tool, from data-driven non-profit newsroom The Mark Up, does show in real time how very different hashtags, groups and news stories are presented by the Facebook recommendation algorithm to The Mark Up's panel of Biden and Trump voters[3].

Twitter may be a slightly more nuanced environment than other online news-gathering scenarios.

There's a brilliant data visualization of more than half a million US tweets, from a 2017 study, illustrating tweeting patterns by political affiliation[4]. Representing left- and right-leaning tweeters as millions of blue and red dots that cluster together densely as two huge blue and red blobs on either side of a big white space, there's only the faintest trail of coloured dots (tweets) linking the two large clusters. It shows how tweets are being widely retweeted within their own political spheres – rarely escaping their colour-coded political bubbles online. But this research particularly looked at tweets on contentious subjects such as gun control, same-sex marriage and climate change. Maybe it just shows that topics that inspire a strong emotional reaction reinforce our polarization online?

Another study on Twitter in the US found that if people on Twitter were deliberately exposed to tweets from people of the opposite political persuasion, their attitudes actually began to harden and they became even more polarized and entrenched in their opposing camps (something about reading their words

Our ▬▬▬▬▬ social media ▬▬ ▬▬▬ feed ▬▬▬▬▬ is ▬▬▬ just ▬▬▬ giving ▬▬▬▬▬▬ ▬▬▬ us ▬▬ the ▬▬▬▬▬▬ news ▬ we ▬▬▬▬▬ want

Only one out of five 👤👤👤👤👤 Facebook friends 👍 will have 👎 opposing views without hearing their voices may be playing out here too, see 'Elephants in the Zoom', page 196)[5].

The filter bubble issue is a complicated one. The jury is still out to some extent on whether they actually exist, whether they only exist on certain platforms, or whether they are just a convenient excuse for the fact that we like to spend time with people who think like us (both online, and off).

So, what was going on online for those London City bankers in the seminar room that day, in the run-up to the EU vote? Was it the case that they were enthusiastically sharing Remain posts with all their friends and connections, who thought and felt just like them, in exactly the same way they would have been doing offline? Or was it the case that some kind of magnification was going on and their filter bubbles were subtly emphasizing and reinforcing their view of the world? (In the Brexit case, there were of course offline polls which were predicting a Remain outcome too, as well as alleged Russian interference, further complicating this particular scenario.)

We may never know, or at least we may not know quite yet. Like so much about the breakneck speed in which the digital revolution has unfolded, things are moving so fast that research into our behaviour online, and convincing explanations for it, are lagging behind. What seeking out our own 'tribe' online of those who share our interests and passions, and only engaging with tweets from those who reflect back our political views both demonstrate is that our will can decide our own reality. It's easy for us to surround ourselves online with opinions that are identical to our own. In doing so, we're increasingly losing touch with the views of others to the point where we're fearful of meaningful debate. Anything that challenges our viewpoint is immediately seen as wrong and shocking. It's time to seek out alternative ideas, challenge ourselves and engage with others. Let's burst the bubble and stop self-aggrandizing views which we know will be met with the applause of others in our bubble. We need to acknowledge the system and demand a better one.

Filter Bubbles:

n. a state of intellectual isolation
when algorithms dictate what you
see online, perfectly matching your
existing views and beliefs.

⚠ SIGNS:

Solely seeing and hearing views and opinions you agree
with, and being notably sheltered from opposing beliefs
and perspectives. Posts in your feed which garner lots of
'yes!' 'THIS' and other verbal applause and endorsements
are a giveaway.

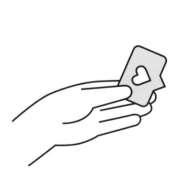

☀ SOLUTION:

If you'd like to widen your world view and break out of your little bubble of those who think exactly like you, you may need to fox the algorithms. I actually find confounding my personal algorithm quite fun to do. One way to do it is to make sure you don't like, follow or comment on any page or content, ever. This is a hard-line approach and can be very tricky to keep up (you will eventually cave when something either truly wonderful or really appalling pops up in your feed). The alternative is to like and follow pages and accounts that are the complete opposite of your own views, alongside liking and following the ones that are. Seek out people online from different cultures, religions and life experiences. Share tweets you disagree with, comment on accounts you'd never normally follow. If algorithms get confused by your seemingly contradictory views and tastes, and really don't know what box to put you in, or what content to serve up or suggest to you, you may be left alone to make your own way online. Just don't be surprised if everything online reinforces your view of the world in your life offline – the digital world isn't magic.

ON ELEPHANTS IN THE ZOOM

'You're on mute!'

The teacher's eye kept being drawn back to one of the little squares in the far-right corner of her online history lesson. The girl in it was bobbing up and down, her face coming in and out of focus and it looked like she was in some kind of wind tunnel. Her hair was blowing around and she looked like she might be out of breath.

'Sophie, are you all right?' she asked. 'What on earth is going on?'

'Sorry Mrs Henderson, I'm having my riding lesson! Mum forgot and booked it in during lesson time, so I brought my phone with me.'

When the teacher told me the story, I couldn't stop laughing. The teacher said she'd had difficulty keeping a straight face too and had suggested Sophie logged off to focus on her riding, saying she would talk to her later.

'A Zoom lesson from the back of a horse was a one-off but we saw and heard all sorts during our online teaching.'

Several times pupils had got up from their chairs to grab a book to reveal they had their pyjama bottoms on underneath their school shirts, and on a couple of occasions only their underwear. And parents talking, or even rowing, loudly in the background was sometimes difficult to avoid overhearing.

We had initially rushed towards mass video calls at the start of the pandemic because we thought it could best replicate the experience of meeting up with each other face to face. Video call platform providers will tell you that's exactly what they do, but like so much technology, it provides a partial substitute and comes with its own set of problems.

There are plenty of examples of how we all have struggled with the etiquette and practicalities of video calls. In one infamous case, a BBC news interview with Professor Robert Kelly was interrupted by his toddler daughter bursting into his study accompanied by her baby brother scooting in on his wheeled baby walker. Their mother dashed in after them and tried to drag them both out of the door under the line of sight of the camera but was fully visible on the screen throughout as she backed out slowly, clutching both of them by the hem of their clothes.

FaceWine (drinks via FaceTime), endless Zoom quizzes and unsightly camera angles stalked our lockdown existence, along with technical incompetence and calls of, 'You're on mute!'

It was a huge learning curve, getting to grips with technology that might have been around for a while but wasn't something we all felt immediately comfortable using all day, every day. Soon enough, everyone complained about being 'Zoomed-out'. And in fact, in March 2021, the Stanford Virtual Human Interaction Lab confirmed that 'Zoom Fatigue' is a real psychological effect caused by 'non-verbal overload'[1]. Zoom said they hosted over 300 million people a day in video meetings in 2020, compared to the 10 million a day they were averaging at the end of 2019[2]. Nearly one-third of Brits in one survey at the end of 2020 said they felt like they'd spent more time than was necessary on video calls[3]. The novelty had definitely worn off.

Video calls are not the same as seeing someone in person, they don't offer the same visual cues that translate into significant communication improvement. Instead, they exhaust and blur boundaries. I'm not singling out Zoom here, whether you're on Microsoft Teams, Google Hangouts or FaceTime, the issues are the same. Viewing yourself constantly on the screen while talking is particularly awkward and stressful – something Stanford dubbed in their research as akin to holding an 'all day mirror' (though some software gives you the option to turn off the 'self-view'). Prolonged close-up eye-to-eye contact with others feels unnatural and threatening. Reading the body language of others on the call is much harder on a screen so you have to work harder to 'read the room'; audio quality isn't as good so you have to strain to listen; and there's the pressure that comes from being permanently visible, which means you can't look away or let your attention wander. Only 12 per cent of employees, in one survey from the US, say they feel as comfortable on video calls as they do on audio[4], and social video calls have similar issues.

The answer is switching back to good old-fashioned phone calls.

YOU'RE ON MUTE

Only **12%** of us feel as comfortable on video calls as on audio

Professor Juliana Schroeder's research is on the psychological processes that underlie social interactions at the Haas School of Business at the University of California, Berkeley. She's studied the impact of voice communication versus visual cues in both workplace feedback and political conversations. One of her studies showed that when you disagree with someone politically you are less critical of them when you hear their voice than when they write something, but then if you add in the option of seeing them via video it doesn't make much difference to how you feel either way. A 2017 Yale study on empathy and voice found that listening to a recorded conversation of people talking, without the video, resulted in a much better understanding of how those people were really feeling, than when video was also added[5].

Video calls can be a total joy when we make the conscious choice to use them to catch up with relatives or friends living far away. Seeing those friendly faces in person can really cheer us up. But making video the default in every situation, when audio would do, is only stressing us out. So, unless we're students studying at home, we can take this pressure off ourselves and substitute some of our video calls for a few old-fashioned audio calls. Not only will it be less tiring, but our communication won't be any poorer for it, it may even be enhanced.

Zoom calls [aka video calling]:

n. video chatting via computer or smartphone using the device's built-in camera.

⚠ SIGNS:

Using your computer or smartphone to make video calls, perhaps over-enthusiastically, when other forms of communication may be possible, even desirable.

☀️ SOLUTION:

Think before every video call. Ask yourself if this needs to be video, or whether audio is enough. If video is the best option, choose your location carefully, to avoid your background being distracting to everyone else on the call. Make sure everyone else at home, or at work, knows you are on a live video call. Lock doors if possible, make signs if not. Dress appropriately. Getting into 'work clothes' for example immediately gets you into the right frame of mind for a work call. If you're only smart from the waist up, make absolutely sure you have everything at your fingertips, so you won't have to stand up mid-call. Check your camera angles and lighting so that you can be seen clearly and are not at an unfortunate angle. Turn off the 'self view' during calls if you can, as this has been shown to be the most stressful aspect of video calling. Check audio and video settings so you're not muted (unless you want to be) before you join the call. Keep video calls short and don't over-commit yourself. I find three video calls in any one day to be about the maximum before Zoom fatigue sets in. There's no research yet to support this number, you have to find what's right for you (your sore eyes will probably tell you when your limit is). If you have to use Zoom, perhaps ask to turn your video off every now and then so it's audio-only, try and take breaks where you can, don't schedule back-to-back calls and avoid multi-tasking whilst on the call.

HOW TO BE A GOOD DIGITAL CITIZEN

The Five **HACCK** Principles

HUMANITY

'We are all connected'

AUTHENTICITY

'I'm always my real self'

COLLABORATION

'Together we achieve more than alone'

CRITICAL THINKING

'I question everything'

KINDNESS

'I treat everyone with compassion'

The internet may be a network of connected computers dominated by Big Tech, but it is also all of us, the users. We can make real and lasting changes if we each use it with a clear set of principles for digital citizenship. This is how we stop waiting and start cleaning up the digital world, together. This manifesto is about making the internet a better place, rather than answering everything explored in this book. If we are going to continue engaging online, we must ask ourselves how we can build, contribute to and maintain a better tomorrow for our digital world.

Join me in my mission. Take the HACCK principles on the previous page – copy them, pin them up on walls, at home, in classrooms, in offices. Add to them, edit them, make them fit your life. But, please, use them.

#1 HUMANITY

'We are all connected.'

In Chinese there is a word, 公德心 *gong de xin*, which loosely translated means the idea of civility, combined with a sense of public spirit. It's about recognizing not only that we are all connected, but that everything I do affects you and everything you do affects me.

Tim Berners-Lee's Contract For The Web, launched in 2019 on the 30th anniversary of the birth of the World Wide Web in 1989, says, 'Everyone has a role to play in safeguarding the future of the Web,' and it's our duty as digital citizens to do so.

In Ancient Greece, the privileges of citizenship also came with a duty and responsibility to contribute to the *polis* (city-state).

Citizens were required to fight in defence of the *polis* and expected to participate in its political life by voting. All Greeks understood that in return for being a citizen you were obliged to do your part in protecting the *polis*, and in determining how it was governed. Inspirational Digital Minister Audrey Tang, an open-source software programmer and the first transgender and non-binary official in the cabinet, says: 'We shouldn't forget about why the internet starts with an "inter" – it's because it allows different policies, different philosophies and different cultures to interconnect.'

Under Audrey, citizens are actively encouraged to view the internet as a space they can all contribute to. A digital citizen participation platform, and its deliberation tool *Pol.is*, is one of the initiatives Audrey has spearheaded. Through the platform, widely diverse groups, from members of the public to government ministers, business leaders and civil society organizations, take part in large-scale discussions on pressing issues and reach a consensus on the solutions.

If being a good citizen offline today includes paying taxes, picking up litter and obeying the law, how can we create a common understanding of what the digital version of a good citizen is?

The HACCK starting point is recognizing that our humanity underlines our connectedness in the digital world. With our sense of common humanity comes an understanding that we all have a vested interest, but also a responsibility, for how the digital world develops and for making it a safe, respectful, positive space. We may not have created all the problems we encounter, but we can contribute to the solutions. It's our town square.

#2 AUTHENTICITY

'I'm always my real self.'

The 'LinkedIn, Facebook, Tinder, Instagram' meme (originating from Dolly Parton no less) that invites everyone to share their different 'faces' on each of those four platforms, is a brilliant way of illustrating how we all show slightly different aspects of ourselves in different locations online.

Authenticity versus anonymity online is a subject that tends to divide people into two distinct camps, each feeling very passionately about their own perspective. In the early days of the internet, anonymity was part of the culture with offline IDs and online profiles often having very little to connect them. When social media switched to a culture focused more on images than words, that habit started to die out a little. But each major platform still allows varying degrees of user anonymity, Twitter and Instagram much more than Facebook for example. And 4chan, which has been entirely built on anonymity, still averages over 900,000 daily posts from its 20 million monthly users.

The anonymous aspect of the digital world, however, is how its most unpleasant behaviours have been able to flourish. There might be many reasons why you too want to remain anonymous online. In some countries of the world, members of the LGBTQ+ community are at risk of being prosecuted and imprisoned for identifying themselves. And for users under 18, some degree of identity protection is essential. In Japan, a country that values personal privacy and low self-disclosure, many social media users still use pseudonyms or even create multiple fake accounts for their online activities, for purely cultural reasons.

But for the majority of us, putting authenticity as a basic principle of being a good digital citizen recognizes the importance of all of us representing ourselves as who we really are in the digital world. If we all did this one thing, we would eliminate trolling (see page 110), romance fraud (see 'Catfishing', page 66) and most online harassment in one stroke.

We must go further. This is not just about not using anonymous accounts or fake profiles, it's also about showing the unvarnished truth in everything we post. We must do away with filters and airbrushing, reject the idea of ideal lives and perfect bodies. The link between the toxic comparison culture online and mental health issues is something we can all play a part in eliminating (see page 86).

In the talks I do in schools I ask children and young people to think about the 't-shirt rule'. If you wouldn't post words or images online that you wouldn't also be happy to put on a t-shirt and wear around those who know and love you, associating your online actions clearly with your face and identity – don't do it. In being authentic we must own every contribution we make to the digital world and be proud to do so.

#3 COLLABORATION

'Together we achieve more
than alone.'

The power of the digital world to connect communities who may be geographically dispersed, to amplify voices who may be silenced and to ignite global movements is one of its most miraculous aspects. To get the very best out of our incredible connectivity, we should focus on how we can use it to come together; to create art, solve problems, to eliminate barriers. Crowdsourcing some of our global or community problems to the internet and finding innovative and creative solutions among the millions of its connected users, has been one of the incredible strengths of our digitally connected world.

A perfect example of when crowdsourcing and collaboration works beautifully for the common good lies right at the heart of our internet, in Wikipedia. Wikipedia's tiny workforce of just ten full-time employees is bolstered by an enthusiastic army of millions of volunteer editors worldwide who create most of the content. Wikipedia actively encourages its users to edit and contribute and has helped them in self-policing any problems or abuses of the system. Yes, it has had its critics, but who reading this can't say that they haven't ever gone to Wikipedia to help them out with information on a topic they can't find anywhere else?

Online collaboration can achieve miraculous things in the real world, too. As on one single day in May 2008 when 50,000 Estonians cleaned up their country in 24 hours. The *'Teeme Ära!'* ('Let's Do It!') campaign, started by Ahti Heinla and Rainer Nolvak, mobilized Estonians first by using GPS and Google Maps to plot the location of over 10,000 illegal rubbish dumpsites, adding detailed descriptions and photos. Then, calling for a mass clean-up in one day. It was the inspiration for the now annual World Cleanup Day.

So, if you have a project, a goal, an ambition, a cause, think about how you can use the digital world to mobilize and inspire others to help make it happen. Set up online groups and websites, use photography, videos and messaging to raise awareness. If you see others initiating projects that support your community or benefit the global good, amplify them, share them and add your voice. This is the one time when you should share and post and retweet and comment without any of the restrictions I've mentioned elsewhere in the book.

#4 CRITICAL THINKING

'I question everything.'

A lot has been written about the importance of critical thinking, but we shouldn't over-complicate it. It comes down to one simple question we need to keep asking ourselves: 'How do I know if this is true?'

I'm not going to get into the realm of 'alternative facts' or alternative truths. Even allowing for nuance and the interpretation of different perspectives, I am starting from the position where we take for granted that objective facts exist, and that we can prove them.

To thrive online, and to be good digital citizens, means to approach everything and everyone with a critical mindset. We must keep asking ourselves questions about the motives and agendas of everyone in the digital space that we don't know personally (that's 99.999 per cent of them), which includes those with a blue tick by a name, or a following in the tens of millions.

For every post, link and share we see, we have to ask a series of questions. What does the original poster have to gain from this? Are they trying to persuade me to do something that will benefit them? Where's the evidence for what they are saying? Have I tried to find an alternative viewpoint? This could get exhausting if we had to do this for every piece of material we come across, every time we go online. Luckily, once we start building up evidence, we can become more confident about who to trust.

One of the most critical looks you can take at any piece of material, app or content is assessing how its owner or publisher makes money. That should give you some pretty big clues about how much you should trust it, or how wary you should be.

It should become second nature to not lazily accept at face value everything we come across online. We must critically appraise everything. And we must be especially careful about repeating or sharing material that we haven't verified to be true. Truth and facts are being debased in the digital world with dangerous results (remember 'Catfishing', see page 66). We must all restore their value.

#5 KINDNESS

'I treat everyone with compassion.'

Unfortunately, not everyone is kind online.

Despite #BeKind hashtags trending regularly on Twitter and Instagram, the digital world can be a hostile and threatening space for many users as some of the stories (particularly 'Trolling', see page 110) in the book have shown.

In lots of ways, modern life itself has made us a lot less kind. We tend not to live in lifelong, close-knit communities anymore where our actions have consequences that we will have to live with. But there can be no doubt that the lack of any real sense of accountability online is at the root of why so very many people are hostile, attacking or just rude to each other in the digital world.

Would I say this to your face? is one thing to ask ourselves when we're firing off a volley of angry tweets, hitting send on an impatient email or furiously typing an aggrieved text. It's one of the most important questions to ask, and the answer is nearly always 'No'.

'*Are you OK?*' is something to ask of other people when we see them being attacked, harassed or bullied online. Feeling that they are not alone, that someone else has noticed what is going on could make a big difference.

'*I love what you are doing*' is always a welcome thing to hear, by anyone working in any field or endeavour. Positive comments bolster people up and may come just at the time they were thinking about giving up on their project or work.

The bedrock of being a good digital citizen, the one principle that must underline all the others, means we must treat everyone we encounter online with kindness. We never know what anyone else is going through, what battles they are fighting, what's really going on behind that glossy social media exterior.

ENDNOTES

LOVING

On Technoference:

1. AVG, 2015, 6,000 8–13yr olds from Brazil, Australia, Canada, France, UK, Germany, The Czech Republic and USA.
2. McDaniel & Radesky, 2017, 170 US two-parent families with children aged over 3 years.
3. Ibid.

On Phadultery:

1. American Academy of Matrimonial Lawyers, 2010.
2. Italian Association of Matrimonial Lawyers, 2014.
3. Lake Legal, USA, 2018.

On Fake News:

1. 'Social Clicks: What and Who gets read on Twitter?', Gabielkov, Columbia University and French National Institute, 2016.
2. 'How People Read Online: The Eyetracking Evidence', Nielsen Norman, 2018.
3. The spread of true and false news online, Dartmouth University, 2018.
4. 'The Spread of True and False News Online', MIT Sloan School of Management, 2018.
5. Industrialized Disinformation 2020, Oxford Internet Institute.
6. Exposure to untrustworthy websites in the 2016 U.S. election, Guess, Nyhan & Reifler, 2019.
7. Fake news, fast and slow: Deliberation reduces belief in false (but not true) news headlines, Bago, Rand & Pennycook 2020.

On Flaky Friends:

1. OnePoll for Evite, 2017.
2. The Economist and The Kaiser Family Foundation (KFF), 2018.
3. B. Primack, University of Pittsburgh, 1,787 US adults, 2014.
4. OnePoll for Pernod-Ricard, 3,000 adults, 2019.

On Sharenting:

1. *Wall Street Journal*, 'The Facebook-Free Baby', May 2012.
2. Ofcom, 2017.
3. Nominet and ParentZone 'Sensible Sharing' study.
4. AVG/Research Now, 2,200 mothers with children under two (EU, Canada, USA, Australia, NZ and Japan).
5. Family Online Safety Institute, 'Parents, Privacy & Technology Use', November 2015.
6. Barclays Bank, 'Sharenting Cost of Data Losses', 2018.
7. Australian Children's eSafety Commissioner, 2015.

On Phubbing:

1. YouGov, 2019, 2,000 adults surveyed.
2. Baylor University, 2017, 450 adults.
3. Bank of America Trends in Consumer Mobility, 2016, 1,000 adults.
4. Partner phubbing and depression among married Chinese adults: The roles of relationship satisfaction and relationship length, 2017.

On Catfishing:

1. Federal Trade Commission, 2019.
2. Action Fraud.

3. Aviva Insurance.
4. Action Fraud.

On Digital Legacies:
1. Digital Death Survey, 2014.
2. 'Are the Dead Taking Over Facebook?', *Öhman and Watson*, 2019.
3. YouGov, 2018.

LIVING

On Comparison Culture:
1. Girls Day School Trust, 5,000 teens, 2017.
2. 'Social comparison, social media and self-esteem', Erin Vogel, University of California, 2014.
3. 'They are happier and having better lives than I am': The impact of using Facebook on perceptions of others' lives. Cyberpsychology, Behaviour, and Social Networking, Chou & Edge, 2012, Utah Valley University.
4. Let me take a selfie: Exploring the psychological effects of posting and viewing selfies and groupies on social media, Wang, Yang, Haig, 2017.

On Multi-Screening:
1. Nielsen Total Audience Report 2018.
2. Linda Stone, 1998.

On Gaming Addiction:
1. www.researchandmarkets.com, 2020.
2. Pew Research 'Gaming and Gamers, 2015, 2,000 adults 18+'.
3. Entertainment Software Association, 'Essential Facts About The Computer and Video Gaming Industry', 2014.
4. Internet Gaming Disorder: Investigating the Clinical Relevance of a New Phenomenon, Przybylski, 2016.

5. Zendle, David, et al. 'The Changing Face of Desktop Video Game Monetisation: An Exploration of Trends in Loot Boxes, Pay to Win, and Cosmetic Microtransactions in the Most-played Steam Games of 2010-2019.' PsyArXiv, 1 Nov. 2019
6. China's Web Junkies: Internet Addiction Documentary, YouTube, *New York Times*, 2014.

On Trolling:
1. Statista 'Internet Usage in the UK', 2020.
2. Ofcom, 'Adults Media Use and Attitudes'.
3. Statista.
4. YouGov, Omnibus, 2014.
5. Online Harms Whitepaper, UK. Gov.
6. Amnesty International, IPSOS/MORI, 2017, Women aged 18–55 in Denmark, Italy, New Zealand, Poland, Spain, Sweden, the UK and USA.
7. Ibid.
8. Ibid.
9. Ibid.

On Vampire Shoppers:
1. Argos, 2018.
2. Barclaycard, 2016.
3. John Lewis Partnership, 2019.
4. One Poll for Gekko, 2,000 UK adults.
5. Money And Mental Health Policy Institute 2019.

On the Quantified Self:
1. Pew Research, June 2019.
2. Ericsson ConsumerLab, Wearable Technology and the Internet of Things, 2016.
3. Internet and smartphone application usage in eating disorders: A descriptive study in Singapore, Tan, Kuek, Goh, Lee, & Kwok, 2016.
4. Calorie counting and fitness tracking

technology: Associations with eating disorder symptomatology, Simpson and Mazzeo, 2017.

5. Factors associated with changes in subjective wellbeing immediately after urban park visit, Yuen and Jenkins, 2019.

On Smombies:

1. Nasar & Troyer, Ohio State University, 2013.
2. Pedestrian Traffic Fatalities by State: 2016 Preliminary Data, US Governors Highway Safety Association.
3. Nasar & Troyer, Ohio State University, 2013.
4. Ambulatory cell phone injuries in the United States: An emerging national concern, Daniel C Smith, *Journal of Safety Research*, 2013.

On Cyberchondria:

1. Pew Research Centre, Health Online, 2013.
2. Fox S. Online Health Search, 2006.
3. Ibid.
4. Statnews.com, 2019.
5. Balance Activ, 2012.
6. Medicalxpress.com, 2017.

LEARNING

On Tech-Life Balance:

1. Opinion Matters, 2013, 503 employees in US workplaces.
2. One Poll for Vision Council, 2,000 American working adults, 2019.
3. Ibid.
4. HubSpot 2020 Remote Work Report, 1,000 adults, US, UK, Germany, Ireland and Austria.

On Doomscrolling

1. Stress in America Survey, Harris Poll for American Psychological Association, 2017.
2. 'The psychological impact of negative TV news bulletins: The catastrophizing of personal worries', Graham Davey, 2011.
3. 'Media use and acute psychological outcomes during COVID-19 outbreak in China', Chao, Xue, 2021.
4. Consumer Demand for Cynical and Negative News Frames, Trussler and Soroka, McGill, 2014.
5. Gerbner, George, 'The "Mainstreaming" Of America: Violence Profile No. 11', 1980

On Clicktivism:

1. www.digiactive.org, 2009.
2. 'From Slacktivism to Activism' Foreign Policy, Morozov, 2009.
3. Five Ways to Wellbeing, New Economics Foundation, 2008.

On Nomophobia:

1. SecurEnvoy 2012, 1,000 US adults in employment.
2. 'An Individual's Growing Fear of Being without a Smartphone', Rodríguez-García, University of Granada, 2020.

On Filter Bubbles:

1. Political polarization on Facebook www.brookings.edu/blog/techtank/2015/05/13/political-polarization-on-facebook.
2. What kind of news gatekeepers do we want machines to be? Filter bubbles, fragmentation, and the normative dimensions of algorithmic recommendations, Nechustai & Lewis, 2019.
3. www.themarkup.org/citizen-browser/2021/03/11/split-screen?feed=biden_trump

4. Emotion shapes the diffusion of moralized content in social networks, Brady, 2017.
5. Exposure to opposing views on social media can increase political polarization, Ball et al, 2018.

On Elephants in the Zoom:
1. tmb.apaopen.org/pub/nonverbal-overload/release/1
2. Business of Apps, 2020.
3. LoopUp, 2020.
4. 'Voice Only Communication Enhance Empathic Accuracy', Michael W. Kraus, Yale, 2017.
5. Bayfields Opticians & Audiologists, 2020.

RESOURCES

ACADEMIC DEPARTMENTS & THINK TANKS

The Citizen Lab: www.Citizenlab.ca – an interdisciplinary laboratory based at the Munk School of Global Affairs & Public Policy, University of Toronto, focusing on research, development, and high-level strategic policy and legal engagement at the intersection of information and communication technologies, human rights and global security.

Oxford Internet Institute:
www.oii.ox.ac.uk – a multidisciplinary research and teaching department of the University of Oxford, dedicated to the social science of the internet.

Oxford University Digital Ethics Lab:
www.digitalethicslab.oii.ox.ac.uk – part of the Oxford Internet Institute - tackling the ethical challenges posed by digital innovation.

The Reuters Institute for the Study of Journalism at Oxford University:
www.reutersinstitute.politics.ox.ac.uk – a research centre and think tank, dedicated to exploring the future of journalism worldwide through debate, engagement and research.

Stanford Digital Civil Society Lab:
www.pacscenter.stanford.edu/research/digital-civil-society-lab – the lab seeks to 'understand, inform, protect and promote civil society in a digitally dependent world'.

Stanford Internet Observatory:
www.cyber.fsi.stanford.edu/io/io – 'a lab housing infrastructure and human expertise for the study of the internet'. A cross-disciplinary program of research, teaching and policy engagement for the study of abuse in current information technologies, with a focus on social media.

Tow Center for Digital Journalism at Columbia University:
www.towcenter.columbia.edu – studying digital journalism, platforms and publishers.

ACTIVISM

The Algorithmic Justice League:
www.ajl.org – a digital advocacy organization in the US, founded by Joy Buolamwini, combining art and research to illuminate the social implications and harms of AI.

Centre for Humane Technology:
www.humanetech.com – US organization founded by ex-Googler Tristan Harris, dedicated to 'radically reimagining our digital infrastructure' with a mission to 'drive a comprehensive shift toward humane technology that supports our well-being, democracy, and shared information environment'.

Foxglove: www.foxglove.org.uk – a non-profit team of lawyers, activists and communication specialists challenging the abuses of power of Big Tech.

Tactical Tech: www.tacticaltech.org – an international NGO that engages with citizens and civil-society organizations to 'explore and mitigate the impacts of technology on society'.

Techinquiry:
www.techinquiry.org/explorer – a 'tech accountability' non-profit founded by Dr Jack Poulson. His work focuses on data curation of the interface between tech companies and weapons manufacturers with the US government and supporting

civil society and tech workers in opposing related abuses.

Time To Log Off: www.itstimetologoff.com – international digital detox and digital wellbeing movement founded by Tanya Goodin, producing resources and research to 'help the screen dependent learn to unplug'.

CYBERCRIME

Action Fraud: www.actionfraud.police.uk – the UK's national reporting centre for fraud and cybercrime.

Consumer Reports' Security Planner:
www.securityplanner.consumerreports.org – produced by non-profit Consumer Reports, the Security Panner will help you cut down on data collection and prevent hackers from invading your laptop, tablet and phone.

CyberCrime Support Network (US):
www.fightcybercrime.org – US nationwide initiative developed to help cybercrime victims through a process of 'Recognize, Report, and Recover' after an incident occurs.

Have I been Pwnd?:
www.haveibeenpwnd.com – a free resource set up by Troy Hunt (a Regional Director of Microsoft), for anyone to assess if their email or phone is in a data breach.

Scamspotter: www.scamspotter.org – a US joint initiative from Google and the CyberCrime Support Network to help consumers spot scams online.

MAKING THE INTERNET SAFE FOR CHILDREN

5Rights Foundation:
www.5rightsfoundation.com – a charity that exists to make systemic changes to the digital world that will ensure it caters for children and young people, by design and default, so that they can thrive.

Common Sense Media:
www.commonsensemedia.org/homepage – produces age-based media reviews for families.

Safer Internet Day:
www.saferinternetday.org/about – from cyberbullying to social networking to digital identity, each year Safer Internet Day aims to raise awareness of emerging online issues and current concerns.

ONLINE ABUSE & HARASSMENT

Anti-Bullying from The Diana Award:
www.antibullyingpro.com – an online resource centre for young people, parents and educators to turn to for issues around bullying behaviour.

Cybersmile Foundation:
www.cybersmile.org – a non-profit committed to tackling all forms of bullying and abuse online.

Glitch: www.fixtheglitch.org – a UK based charity founded by Seyi Akiwowo, working to make the online space safe for all by raising awareness of online abuse and its impact through an intersectional lens.

ORGANIZATIONS PROMOTING THE GLOBAL, OPEN, SHARED RESOURCES OF THE INTERNET

Ada Lovelace Institute:
www.adalovelaceinstitute.org – an independent research institute and deliberative body with a mission to ensure data and AI work for people and society.

Contract for the Web:
www.contractfortheweb.org – produced by the World Wide Web Foundation, a global plan of action to make the online world safe and empowering for everyone

Open Data Institute: www.theodi.org – co-founded in 2012 by the inventor of the web Sir Tim Berners-Lee and Artificial Intelligence expert Sir Nigel Shadbolt to advocate for the innovative use of open data to affect positive change across the globe.

Wikimedia Foundation:
www.wikimediafoundation.org – the non-profit which hosts 13 collaborative knowledge projects from Wikipedia, the free encyclopaedia, to Wikidata, a set of structured data, and beyond.

World Wide Web Foundation:
www.webfoundation.org – Founded by Tim Berners-Lee to advance the open web as a public good and a basic right.

PODCASTS

It's Complicated – hosted by Tanya Goodin.

Your Undivided Attention – hosted by
· Tristan Harris and Aza Raskin.

REPORTING ON BIG TECH

The Markup: www.themarkup.org – a
non-profit newsroom that investigates how
powerful institutions are using technology
to change society.

Protocol: www.protocol.com – a new
media company from the publisher of
POLITICO, focusing on the 'people, power
and politics of tech'.

Recode at Vox: www.vox.com/recode –
uncovering and explaining how our digital
world is changing — and changing us.

TACKLING MISINFORMATION

BBC Reality Check:
www.bbc.co.uk/news/reality_check – fact-
checking specialist unit within the BBC, fact-
checking trending news stories of the day.

The Centre for Countering Digital Hate:
www.counterhate.com – an international
not-for-profit NGO that seeks to disrupt
the architecture of online hate and
misinformation. Offices in London and
Washington DC.

First Draft News: www.firstdraftnews.org
– an organisation working 'to empower
society with the knowledge, understanding,
and tools needed to outsmart false and
misleading information'.

FullFact: www.fullfact.org – the UK's
independent fact-checking charity.

Lumen: www.lumendatabase.org – Lumen
is an independent research project of
the Berkman Klein Center for Internet &
Society at Harvard University, studying
'cease and desist' letters on online content.

Poynter Institute: www.poynter.org –
home of the International Fact-Checking
Network (IFCN) which sets a code of ethics
for fact-checking organizations.

INDEX

ACKNOWLEDGEMENTS

With grateful thanks to all the professionals, academics and individuals who helped and informed me with the research for the book, having been in many cases originally guests on my podcast: Seyi Akiwowo, Max Benwell, Debbie Chism, Emily Cummin, Dr Richard Graham, Dr Sophie Jukes, Professor Guy Leschziner, Professor Sonia Livingstone OBE FBA, Professor Juliana Schroeder and Professor David Veale. Thanks too to both the Oxford Internet Institute and the Reuters Institute for the Study of Journalism at Oxford University, both world-leading centres of research whose reports and research are referenced in this book.

Thank you to my editor Zara Anvari who always takes my book concepts and polishes them into a far more articulate and concise version of anything I could produce on my own.

Thank you to Andrew Syer and Sophie Hanscombe again, for love, support, proof-reading and sense-checking.

Quite serendipitously, the copy for this book was delivered on my late father's birthday and will be published on my late godfather's. Both were major influences on me. Both were engineers and technophiles, who inspired me to go into a field that wasn't typical for a woman at the time, without giving it a second thought and with great confidence that I could succeed. So, thank you to Peter Goodin and Ron Short, I owe you both a tremendous amount.

About the Author

Tanya Goodin is the founder of digital detox movement Time To Log Off, an author, speaker and campaigner on tech ethics, and host of the 'It's Complicated' podcast. She consults for companies, organisations, individuals and families on the healthy use of technology.

She has appeared on *BBC Breakfast*, Sky News, CCTV (China State TV), ITN London News, BBC Radio 4 *Today* programme, BBC's *Woman's Hour*, ITV National News and the BBC World Service. Her articles can be found in *The Guardian*, *The Telegraph*, *London Evening Standard*, *Marie Claire*, *The Daily Mail* and *The Sun*.

Follow Tanya on Twitter @tanyagoodin and Instagram @timetologoff, and visit her websites tanyagoodin.com and itstimetologoff.com.